The Moonlight Sonata of Beethoven Blatz

The
Moonlight Sonata
of **Beethoven Blatz**

Armin Wiebe

The Moonlight Sonata of Beethoven Blatz
first published 2011 by
Scirocco Drama
An imprint of J. Gordon Shillingford Publishing Inc.
© 2011 Armin Wiebe

Scirocco Drama Editor: Glenda MacFarlane
Cover design by Terry Gallagher/Doowah Design Inc.
Author photo by Sara Jane Wiebe
Printed and bound in Canada on 100% post-consumer recycled paper.

We acknowledge the financial support of the Manitoba Arts Council and The Canada
Council for the Arts for our publishing program.

Library and Archives Canada Cataloguing in Publication

Wiebe, Armin
    The moonlight sonata of Beethoven Blatz / Armin Wiebe.

A play.
ISBN 978-1-897289-60-0

    I. Title.

PS8595.I3573M66 2011   C812'.54   C2011-901118-2

J. Gordon Shillingford Publishing
P.O. Box 86, RPO Corydon Avenue, Winnipeg, MB Canada R3M 3S3

To Mildred Wiebe 1944-2009

Acknowledgements

I must thank Rory Runnells, godfather of playmaking in Manitoba, for pestering this novelist to write a play; Bruce McManus, Ulla Ryum, and Kim McCaw for their encouragement and dramaturgical insights; Manitoba Association of Playwrights and Prairie Theatre Exchange's Stage Two program, which led to a reading at the Carol Shields Festival of New Works; Ardith Boxall and Rea Kavanagh at Theatre Projects Manitoba who got behind the play early; Lori Lam and Manitoba Theatre Centre; University of Alberta's Working Title new play festival; the workshop actors: Tom Keenan, Patricia Hunter, Gordon Tanner, Kristen Miller, Arne MacPherson, Jacqueline Loewen, Monique Marcker, Kevin Klassen, Krista Jackson, Eric Nyland, Cole Humeny, Elena Porter, and Beth Graham; Manitoba Arts Council and Winnipeg Arts Council for financial support during the writing of this play; Lawrence Scanlon and Karon Sackney for providing horsetail hair for the Brummtopp; Darren Wiebe for composing the initial Blatz's sonata; Susie Moloney for the duet read-through; Ludwig van Beethoven, of course; *Wide Open Windows*, the grade five reader containing the anonymous, mythical story of how Beethoven composed a sonata to the moonlight; and Mildred, my immortal beloved, whose presence and absence has permeated everything I've written.

Playwright's Notes

An anecdote pops into my mind during a writing exercise: my grandfather contracts poison ivy so bad he has to wear a dress in the field to conduct the harvest. I begin musing about grandfather and grandmother choosing the dress. Later, I sit down to write a story, and a grandmother's voice (not *my* grandmother's voice) begins telling the story of her husband (not *my* grandfather). The completed story, published in *Due West* as "And Besides God Made Poison Ivy", leaves me with many unanswered questions and a sense that there is a much bigger story still to be written and that I have characters with significant depths to be plumbed. I also feel a darkness lurking beneath the comic surface that I have not explored in my earlier comic writing. Unlike my previous stories that have wanted to grow into novels, this story wants to be a play, a play with music that may confuse your heart, clapper your bones, and yes, tickle you like may be a snake in the grass and lift you from bread dough in the pan up to white clouds in the sky…and that's just the piano. Lurking in the shadows is the mysterious, sinister, possibly pagan companion of Mennonite New Year's mummers, the Brummtopp.

When I first saw plays in the 1960s the predominant accent on the stage was British, but this play wants to use language tinged with the Flat German of *The Salvation of Yasch Siemens*, that is, buggered up English sprinkled with Mennonite *Plautdietsch* and some High German.

The characters wrestle with doubts and fears as they act on or resist their impulses: Can a man reach to heaven if he never looks to the sky? Can a woman only bake with what a man has to give? Can a woman hunger so much that she will reach where she should not reach? Can a man who hears music in the birds, in the grass, even yet in a snake still ask "matters such a thing"? If people get what they need, if what they get is good, does it still need to bother their heads?

Wanting can be such sweet sorrow, but on the prairies we make it work.

Characters

SUSCH KEHLER:...................... A farm wife, aged 21 (rhymes with "push").

OBRUM KEHLER: .... A farmer/carpenter, aged 28.

TEEN:... A midwife, aged 30.

BEETHOVEN BLATZ:.............. A refugee from the Russian revolution, a musician, aged 35.

Setting

A farmstead on a section of mostly unbroken Manitoba prairie in the 1930s. The action occurs in three areas: a one-room farm house, an adjacent yard, and a prairie field.

Inside the house the action occurs in the kitchen area, the bedroom area, and the piano area.

The set conveys a sense of confinement, oppressive and restrictive, yet expansive like a womb as the play unfolds (cozy poverty, a rustic love nest, hard times with laughter).

Main Props

Upright piano, wood cookstove, table & chairs, bench, hand crank cream separator, bed, straw ticking mattress, washline, a Brummtopp (a friction drum made of a wooden barrel with a skin stretched over the top with a swatch of horsetail hair fastened to the centre of the skin) with a shiny new enamel basin near it. These props would be on stage throughout.

Production History

The Moonlight Sonata of Beethoven Blatz premiered at Theatre Projects Manitoba, Winnipeg,. on April 7, 2011 with the following cast:

BLATZ...Eric Nyland
OBRUM ....Tom Keenan
SUSCH ....Tracy Penner
TEEN...Daria Puttaert

Directed by Kim McCaw
Set Design by Brian Perchaluk
Lighting Design by Hugh Conacher
Musical Direction and Sound Design by Greg Lowe
Dialect Coach: Shannon Vickers
Props and Wardrobe: Elana Honcharuk
Stage Manager: Sheena Sanderson
Apprentice Stage Manager: Lisa Nelson
Producer: Rea Kavanagh
Artistic Director: Ardith Boxall

Armin Wiebe

Armin Wiebe is celebrated for his beloved, lexicon-expanding Gutenthal novels *The Salvation of Yasch Siemens*, *Murder in Guthenthal*, and *The Second Coming of Yeeat Schpanst*. He is also the winner of the McNally Robinson Manitoba Book of the Year Award and the Margaret Laurence Award for Fiction for his novel *Tatsea*.

Act I

Scene 1

> *Sounds of a piano rolling off a wagon and crashing to the ground.*

OBRUM: *(Offstage.)* Dusent noch emol eent!

SUSCH: *(Offstage.)* Obrum, what is this thing?

OBRUM: *(Offstage.)* How could such a thing happen?

SUSCH: *(Offstage.)* You stopped the wheel on my stick roses. The earth is too soft there for such a heavy thing.

OBRUM: *(Offstage.)* This I didn't want at all.

> *SUSCH and OBRUM maneuver the piano over the doorsill and push it across the floor bumping into the Brummtopp as they position it opposite the kitchen area. The front cover is missing from the piano, exposing the inner works. Additional removable items could be missing to add to the impression of a damaged instrument.*

SUSCH: What want you with such a thing here on the farm?

OBRUM: What wants a man with a rainbow in the sky?

SUSCH: A rainbow?

OBRUM: Yes, what wants a man with red and yellow and orange and purple in the sky?

SUSCH: Ach you, let me go!

OBRUM: Why needs a man a woman so soft?

SUSCH: Don't!

OBRUM: Susch, I thought I had learned you to laugh already.

SUSCH: Somebody will see us yet!

OBRUM: If a man can't tickle his wife...weren't you listening at the wedding?

SUSCH: It was all in English so I maybe didn't understand so good.

OBRUM: Yeah, well, we know how come that was...you think it would have been better if Preacher Funk had married us together?

SUSCH: My mother and father and Lisa and Pete could have come and the whole village too.

OBRUM: Do we need a whole village?

SUSCH: Obrum Kehler, you bring home a broken thing right into this woodbox we have in to live.

OBRUM: Oh yes, that.

SUSCH: What will you do with it?

          A thunderclap.

OBRUM: Beethoven.

SUSCH: What?

OBRUM: Blatz. Beethoven Blatz.

          OBRUM rushes off.

SUSCH: What wants he now?

SUSCH is drawn to the piano. Timidly she presses a key, then another, but startled by the movement of the hammers inside, she gets confused and stops.

OBRUM carries in the piano cover.

OBRUM: Here, take this. I must bring in the bench yet.

SUSCH takes the cover and carries it over to the piano, holds it up as if to close the piano, but curiosity takes over and she leans the cover against the piano and presses keys again to watch the hammers hitting the strings.

OBRUM carries in the piano bench and sets it down behind SUSCH and wipes the seat off with his sleeve.

Sit, Susch.

OBRUM embraces SUSCH as he gently pushes her to sit on the bench with him.

Let's play something! It maybe still works.

SUSCH: Obrum, what...?

OBRUM plays 'Chopsticks', ignoring the fact that some keys no longer work or are out of tune.

OBRUM: Here...now you try.

SUSCH: No, I can't play.

OBRUM: Ach, Susch, it's not so hard...here, I'll hold your fingers.

SUSCH: No, I didn't wash my hands.

OBRUM plays 'Chopsticks' very slowly with SUSCH's hands.

OBRUM: See, it's not so hard to do. Let's play through again.

SUSCH: Ach you, isn't one time enough for you? Anyways you said you would bring home a washing machine *(Piano playing.)* Ouch! You pinched my finger!

OBRUM: Here, put your fingers there...then it's like running together *(Plays.)* and then running apart again. *(Plays.)*

SUSCH: OK, let me then already. *(Plays slowly.)*

OBRUM: Good, now a little faster. *(Plays.)* Good, now a little faster.

SUSCH: OK, can I stop now? I must go use the scrub board.

OBRUM: Oh, no, we have to play it together.

SUSCH: I thought we just did.

OBRUM: Oh no, you play on the high keys there and I will play on the low keys here.

SUSCH: How could such a thing work?

OBRUM: Just try it. Play the coming together part. *(SUSCH plays.)* OK, now I will play it, too. *(They play almost together.)* Again. *(They play.)* Now the going apart part. *(They play.)* See?

SUSCH: How come a man knows such things?

OBRUM: Let's play it again, over and over.

SUSCH: Over and over. *(They play, slowly at first, then faster and faster.)* Holem de gruel. *(Dog barks.)*

OBRUM: Good girl, Susch.

> *They play louder, faster, the dog barks, a crow caws, cows moo, the piano and the animals build up a crescendo of sound. OBRUM stops, but SUSCH continues to play, intent on getting it right. OBRUM snuggles up and begins to smooch and*

caress SUSCH, who tries to continue to play, but gives in to the advances and stops.

SUSCH: Obrum, it's not even yet night!

OBRUM: Who will see, here so far from the village?

SUSCH: At least let's go to the bed.

OBRUM continues his smooching as they waltz behind the bedroom curtain in the fading light.

Outside, TEEN hurries on in the rain as if coming to visit. She carries her midwife bag. Amourous sounds. TEEN pauses and gazes at the house as she listens.

OBRUM: *(Offstage.)* Eine kleine Nacht Musik!

TEEN: *(Muttering.)* Nacht Musik, eine kleine Nacht Musik.

TEEN stomps off.

Scene 2

Early morning. Kitchen.

SUSCH enters from bedroom wearing her nightdress.

SUSCH: How come it is…after I let myself go with Obrum Kehler in the night…in the morning always I want to feel the wet grass on my feet? *(SUSCH moves toward the door as if to go outside, but is distracted by the piano.)* Obrum Kehler, what want you from me? Isn't it enough if I pull carrots out of the garden and rub them clean for you? *(She caresses the side of the piano.)* Two years already in your bed and my belly stays flat like the sides of this piano thing. *(Presses a key.)* 'Eine kleine Nachtmusik' you mumbled in the dark. *(Tries to play 'Chopsticks'.)* What Obrum? What mean you with this thing? *(Plays more keys.)*

Bring you this thing because I cannot…even after two years? *(Plays more keys.)* Is this what will be our child? Oh Mensch I'm frightened even to remember it…all the night through I dreamed about those crooked piano keys and they laughed at me like they were peeking at me in the outhouse. You thing you! *(Pounds keys with fist.)* What anyways do you here? I can't wash clothes with you. *(Tries to play 'Chopsticks' again.)* Can pulling carrots be enough?

> *OBRUM, pants over his combination underwear but no shirt, enters carrying cream can and armful of syrup pails.*

OBRUM: Ach yoh, en Engel met Klavier. Such a lucky Mensch.

SUSCH: What want you with those pails?

OBRUM: Blueberries. On the other side of the river. It rained in the night and the thrashers will be late a day. Let's go before they are all picked over.

SUSCH: But I didn't milk yet!

OBRUM: I'll help you, come.

SUSCH: But my nightdress!

OBRUM: I'll blindfold the cows.

SUSCH: No, my milking dress first.

OBRUM: There isn't time.

> *OBRUM starts to drag SUSCH off.*

SUSCH: First a Model T, then a broken piano thing, and now blueberries before breakfast! Can't you ever sit still?

> *SUSCH exits.*

OBRUM: Not with such a woman. *(Plays a key.)* Can a man reach to heaven if he never looks to the sky?

          OBRUM exits.

Scene 3

          Sunrise. On the prairie.

          TEEN strides on carrying midwife bag.

TEEN: *(Muttering.)* Eine kleine Nacht Musik. Eine kleine Nacht Musik.

          BLATZ trudges on from the opposite direction, a bag of tools over his shoulder. TEEN collides with BLATZ, knocking tool bag off his shoulder, and struggles to maintain her balance.

BLATZ: Fraülein Schellenberg! *(BLATZ reaches out to steady TEEN.)* Ist Fraülein, ja...nicht Frau?

TEEN: *(Slaps away his hand.)* A Russian Blatz before sunup yet I don't need.

BLATZ: Nah, nah, Fraülein—

TEEN: Nineteen hours to bring that little Giesbrecht into the world and her man yet wants breakfast ready on the table.

BLATZ: You like not a man to please?

TEEN: A man just has to be cleaned up after.

BLATZ: Ah so, ist Fraülein, nicht Frau.

TEEN: I have no time for this dummheit, by the dark Penners Elsie brings forth her twelfth. *(TEEN strides off, muttering.)* Eine kleine Nacht Musik, eine kleine Nacht Musik.

BLATZ: *(Watches TEEN go.)* Ach Sonya, hab ich kein Herz?

BLATZ reaches inside his bag and pulls out a tuning fork. He sits down on the bag and hits the palm of his hand with the tuning fork and holds it up to his ear.

What is my haste to walk through the night to see a broken Klavier?

He strikes with the tuning fork again, sings in tune with fork.

Doh. *(Strikes fork again, sings.)* Doh, ti, la, so, fa, me, re, doh.

A crow caws as he reaches the lower "doh". BLATZ rises, sings ascending scale.

Caw, caw, caw, caw, caw, caw, caw, caw.

BLATZ tosses the tuning fork back into the bag, hoists the bag to his shoulder. A mourning dove coos as he trudges off.

Scene 4

Next morning. Bedroom. Mourning dove coos. Cream can and syrup pails in kitchen.

OBRUM: *(As if in answer to the mourning dove.)* Ooooo…oo…oooo—

OBRUM jumps out of bed and tears off his combination underwear so the buttons fly.

SUSCH: *(Sitting up in bed.)* What's loose with you?

She laughs as OBRUM dances naked around the room in itchy agony.

What wiped you with yesterday in the bush?

OBRUM: It itches like a thousand mosquito bites.

SUSCH: Don't you know poison ivy when you see it? *(Aside.)* It's good you stayed on your own side of the bed.

> *OBRUM is too tormented to speak. SUSCH breaks up into laughter again. As SUSCH speaks the next lines she changes from night dress to house dress. This should be a modest maneuver that doesn't involve nudity.*

SUSCH: *(Aside.)* I shouldn't laugh, but if it happens to me, Obrum will snort like a horse each time he looks at me for the next ten years.

OBRUM: Susch, help me.

SUSCH: Don't scratch yourself. I must go milk the cows.

> *SUSCH moves into the kitchen area. OBRUM follows her.*

OBRUM: Susch, the thrashers come today. What will I do?

SUSCH: You can't wear pants, they would rub the skin too much.

OBRUM: And I can't go naked to thrash barley.

SUSCH: I'll tell them they have to thrash without you.

OBRUM: No. I just need some kind of clothes that don't rub between the legs.

SUSCH: Even wide pants would rub together and a person can't walk around broad-legged all day.

OBRUM: There must be something…something like…a smooth kind of thing…

SUSCH: *(Laughs.)* A smooth kind of thing *(Laughs.)* that doesn't rub! *(Laughs.)* Ach no, even Obrum Kehler wouldn't …*(Laughs.)*

OBRUM: What?

SUSCH: No…(*Laughs.*)…never such a thing…no.

OBRUM: What? Tell me!

SUSCH: Cover yourself. This isn't the Garden of Eden, you know.

OBRUM: You mean leaves?

SUSCH: Ach no, leaves you tried already! (*Laughs.*)

OBRUM: Tell me, Susch!

SUSCH: No, you could never do it. (*Laughs.*) I'll just tell the thrashers that you are sick.

OBRUM: No, I'm not sick! I just need loose clothes that let the wind blow through.

SUSCH: A woman can wear such a thing, but…

OBRUM: What you mean a woman…oh…I see…(*Sound of threshing crew in the distance.*) Hear you that? Susch, show me what you have!

SUSCH: I don't believe this, no, you stay here. (*Goes into bedroom.*)

OBRUM: Hurry, the thrashers are almost to the yard.

SUSCH: (*Comes out with flowered dress.*) Maybe this will fit. Good thing you are smaller than a woman.

OBRUM: Flowers? No, I need a manly dress.

SUSCH: A manly dress? (*Laughs.*)

OBRUM: Yeah, dark black like my pants.

SUSCH: You should have married a Russian grandmother if you wanted a black dress.

OBRUM: You know, that black thing you use in winter.

SUSCH:	No, Obrum Kehler, not my black wool skirt for thrashing barley.
OBRUM:	That's the one I mean. Go get it.
SUSCH:	I have to cover you up somehow. *(Goes to bedroom to get skirt.)*
OBRUM:	*(Picks up flowered dress and puts it on.)* Feels cool. Doesn't rub. Am I really smaller than a woman?
SUSCH:	*(Enters with black wool skirt. Laughs.)* That dress fits you better than it fits me. How does it feel?
OBRUM:	Not so bad. *(Pulls dress off.)*
SUSCH:	Don't tear it.
OBRUM:	Give me that one. From far off nobody will see.
SUSCH:	You don't want to put this on.

OBRUM puts on wool skirt.

OBRUM:	Eeeeaaash! It scratches like barley!
SUSCH:	I told you.
OBRUM:	Woman I know! *(Takes off skirt.)* Eeeaash!
SUSCH:	It's hot, you need a thin dress.
OBRUM:	I can't wear flowers.
SUSCH:	All my dresses have flowers.
OBRUM:	No. *(He puts one leg back into the wool skirt.)* Eeeaash! *(Steps out again.)* Susch, what use women anyways?
SUSCH:	What mean you?
OBRUM:	Men use underwear, what use women?
SUSCH:	Oh. With an underskirt maybe you could.

SUSCH goes to get underskirt.

OBRUM: Yes, get me an underskirt, then I can wear this black thing with my shirt and from the road it won't look like a dress.

SUSCH: *(Off.)* Let's see which one would fit best.

OBRUM: The white one.

SUSCH: *(Off.)* My underskirts are all white.

OBRUM: The one I brought you for getting married, that should work.

SUSCH: *(Off.)* The wedding underskirt?

OBRUM: Bring it, the thrashing machine comes into the yard.

SUSCH: *(Off.)* You can't do such a thing!

Sounds of threshing crew.

OBRUM: Hurry up, girl!

SUSCH: *(Off.)* No, not from the wedding.

OBRUM: Do I have to get it myself?

SUSCH: *(Off.)* No, Obrum, don't—

OBRUM: Under the black skirt it will stay white.

SUSCH: *(Carrying white silk underskirt.)* Must you?

OBRUM: Just till this itch goes away. *(Puts on underskirt.)*

SUSCH: Don't rip it, a woman gets only one like that in her life.

OBRUM: How come only women can wear such smooth things? *(Pulls on wool skirt. Knocking.)* Hurry, my shirt. *(Calls out window.)* Go to the first field. Yeah, the barley first.

SUSCH: *(Gives him a shirt.)* Here, let me help your arm in. Is the skirt too tight?

OBRUM: No, it's good...mmm...I can feel the air from the wire window blowing up my legs.

SUSCH: *(Laughs.)* And men think they have everything better.

OBRUM: Susch, how do I look?

SUSCH: *(Bracing herself on the Brummtopp.)* Like you're going out with the Brummtopp mummers on New Year's Eve!

OBRUM: I love you Susch and bake the thrashers a blueberry pie for dinner

   OBRUM exits.

SUSCH: Ach you, now yet I have to feed all those men! *(Sits down.)* But my wedding underskirt...*(She laughs nervously.)* Oh...but no...how can I yet laugh when I saw that poison ivy between his legs? What if he can never again...

   BLATZ enters, carrying his tools directly to the piano without noticing SUSCH. BLATZ sets down his bag, reaches out and plays a discordant chord. Beethoven BLATZ opens piano and inspects for damage, plays runs of the scale and cocks his ear to listen for discordance.

   (Whispers.) Who is that? With yet a white shirt and a necktie on a weekday? Still he looks...like a little boy...not quite clean. *(Pause.)* How come it is that I...right now I want to pull that man out of his Sunday suit and scrub him in a washtub? *(Cows moo.)* Gott im Himmel, the cows!

BLATZ: *(Cries out.)* Sonya!

   BLATZ plays a chord that works: opening chord of 'Moonlight Sonata'.

SUSCH: Susch. My name is Susch. Sarah in English if you want but people call me Susch.

          BLATZ's attention is split between Susch and the sound of the piano.

BLATZ: Bitte, I am sorry. Kehler, he speaks double sometimes. His intended truth is not every time clear.

SUSCH: He said you my name is Sonya?

BLATZ: Aber nein, der Kehler…bitte Sonya, uh, Susch, bitte hear once you this.

SUSCH: What mean you?

          BLATZ plays opening arpeggios of 'Moonlight Sonata', but quickly encounters discordant notes and keys that produce no sound at all.

          Mensch, who are you?

          BLATZ ignores her as he continues to play 'Moonlight Sonata', returning to the opening bar again and again playing until he reaches the damaged part of the piano.

\   How come Obrum brought this thing to fall off the wagon by my house?

BLATZ: Das Klavier, oh ja, it is fallen from the wagon and Kehler wants I should make repair. *(He plays part of a scale.)*

SUSCH: Make repair?

BLATZ: Musician Kehler is not. *(Plays arpeggio.)* Aber this woman, she maybe could be learned.

SUSCH: Why talk you like I am not here?

BLATZ: *(Plays opening chord of 'Moonlight Sonata'.)* Aber hear once you this. *(Plays chord again.)* Hope could be. *(Plays chord again.)* Hear once you this.

> *BLATZ plays the opening arpeggios until he hits the damaged section of the keyboard. At this point he hammers on the keys like a demented man creating raucous discordant sounds. When he stops, a dog's barking is heard, a cow moos.*

SUSCH: What? Hear such noise that the cows get frightened and give no milk?

> *BLATZ bangs on the keys again, then plays scales up and down the entire keyboard, ignoring the discordant sounds.*

BLATZ: Hope, hope there could be, aber much work. But Sonya, I hear something in this Klavier, I hear something. Make repair I must.

> *BLATZ pounds on the keys again. SUSCH gets in his face.*

SUSCH: Mensch, you are deaf?

> *BLATZ looks at SUSCH as if seeing her for the first time.*

BLATZ: Fräulein, du bist…you are…really you are…

SUSCH: Nah yoh, I am Kehler's wife, ja?

BLATZ: *(Not hearing her.)* Sonya, mein Liebchen, music there can be again.

> *BLATZ embraces SUSCH. SUSCH is so shocked she doesn't even think to protest, or struggle.*

BLATZ: Sonya, I will please you yet, I will make repair, Sonya—I will yet play a 'Moonlight' worthy of Beethoven.

> *BLATZ swings SUSCH around as if in a dance.*

TEEN ENTERS and stops, startled.

SUSCH: Mensch, what will you with me?

BLATZ again does not hear her and clasps her more tightly to him, bending his cheek to her cheek as he continues the swing. TEEN shocked and jealous.

BLATZ: Sonya, die Kunst is not forever lost. Die Musik…in this poor instrument…I hear it.

BLATZ lets SUSCH go, and she spins dizzily into TEEN's arms, dropping the pails as they collide. TEEN automatically embraces SUSCH. BLATZ rushes back to the piano. TEEN holds on. SUSCH shrugs herself out of TEEN's arms.

SUSCH: Oh but Teen, what do you here?

TEEN: I come help the thrasher gang to feed, but *(Glares at BLATZ.)* maybe too many cooks can spoil the borscht.

SUSCH, flustered, picks up the pails.

SUSCH: I must milk yet. You can pick through some blueberries for dinner.

SUSCH exits.

TEEN: Nah yoh, Blatz, I had heard that in Russia it is getting worldly, but dancing with another man's wife in the middle of a thrashing morning?

BLATZ: And the thrashers need yet a midwife today?

OBRUM enters.

TEEN: Huy, yuy, yuy!

BLATZ bursts out laughing when he sees the dress. TEEN too is amused.

BLATZ: You wear now the dress? So schrecklijch I did not think wedlock would be.

TEEN: Oh, oh.

BLATZ: Or has your boarding school affliction come back?

OBRUM: No, not that, just a bit poison ivy.

BLATZ: But always between the legs with you.

TEEN: Shame yourself!

OBRUM: Ja, Schweinkopf, aber das Klavier, you think you can fix?

BLATZ: Hear once you this.

> BLATZ plays an arpeggio.

OBRUM: So it can still learn Susch piano playing?

TEEN: (Aside.) Susch?

BLATZ: First repair, tutoring could follow.

OBRUM: Chopsticks I can learn her myself, but real music needs musician, not Teen?

TEEN: Nah Obrum, I don't—

BLATZ: A bed I will need…and time.

OBRUM: A bed?

TEEN: But your school, soon it is starting, yes?

BLATZ: Schul? Nein, das Klavier, die Kunst, my art first.

TEEN: Sure bold that Blatz is, even for a Russian.

SUSCH: Sonya…Sonya he called me.

> SUSCH sets milk pails down in front of door.

TEEN: What you say?

SUSCH: Is that a Russian name, Sonya? Or says he Sonny?

TEEN: Sonny? For sure even in Russia a Sonny wouldn't wear a dress.

                OBRUM enters wearing skirt and shirt. SUSCH turns away, embarrassed.

OBRUM: Blatz thinks he can the piano fix.

TEEN: Maybe not in Russia, but in Gutenthal it looks like a Sonny can.

OBRUM: Did Menno Simons wear pants?

                OBRUM stomps off. SUSCH smirks, embarrassed.

SUSCH: *(Forces a laugh.)* What can a woman do with such a man?

                TEEN sets down cream can, puts her hand on SUSCH.

TEEN: A woman who had such a hurry-up wedding should maybe have diapers on her line.

SUSCH: Ach Teen, wanting is such tangled twine.

TEEN: Oh but Susch!

                OBRUM comes on.

OBRUM: Susch, nine thrashers for dinner.

                OBRUM goes off.

SUSCH: Oh Mensch, the thrashers, and Obrum wants yet blueberry pie for dinner.

TEEN: Susch, Susch, whatever you set before them, hungry men will eat.

                BLATZ tries to play 'Moonlight Sonata'.

SUSCH: But it's the woman's failing, not, if it doesn't schmeck so good.

TEEN: A woman can only bake with what a man has to give.

SUSCH: *(Aside.)* Two years already he gives and no dough yet will rise.

TEEN: Anyways, today is too hot for baking. Fresh cream on the blueberries, who will complain? Come, let's sit in the shade to pick them through.

> *BLATZ's piano playing intensifies. BLATZ pounds on faulty keys, opens lid, front of piano, etc. He is frustrated, ready to give up. He closes the keyboard cover and stomps out the door nearly stumbling on the milk pails. Reflexively, he picks up the pails, carries them in, and pours one pail into the separator. He starts to turn the crank, stops, and approaches the piano gingerly and lifts the keyboard cover. He plays the opening chord of 'Moonlight Sonata'. He listens, plays it again.*

BLATZ: I do hear it, Sonya. My ear I must believe, you said. More than my tools I shall need here. Yes. *(BLATZ rummages through his bag and pulls out a sheaf of papers.)* My manuscripts. Ah, never back to that school. Die Schmutzhackende Kinder!

Scene 5

> *The next day. The kitchen area.*
>
> *SUSCH sits at table threading a length of twine through safety pins pinned along the edge of a large sheet.*
>
> *BLATZ tinkers with the piano.*
>
> *SUSCH picks up a hammer and nail and drags a chair into position. She gets up on the chair and hammers a nail into the back wall.*
>
> *BLATZ keeps tinkering. SUSCH steps down,*

gathers up the sheet, gets up on chair again and fastens the end of the twine to the nail. She steps down, and raising the other end of the twine as high as she can, stretches the sheet out so the piano is blocked off from the kitchen area. She lowers the sheet, drags the chair into position again, grabs the end of the twine, gets up on the chair, and stretches up to hook the loop into a hook in the ceiling. She can't quite reach.

SUSCH: Bitte hilf.

SUSCH steps down and holds up the end of the twine for BLATZ. As if puzzled, BLATZ rises from the piano bench. SUSCH steps backward, stumbles into BLATZ. An unconscious embrace that ends with their sitting backwards side by side on the piano bench, leaning lightly on each other. They sit for a moment without speaking, as if in shock. SUSCH starts out of the daze first and looks around.

SUSCH: Mustn't we sit the other way?

BLATZ: Sonya, what mean you?

SUSCH: Susch, I am Susch, mein dummer Herr. Aber to play Klavier, mustn't we sit the other way? The piano thing is behind.

BLATZ: Play Klavier? *(He looks over his shoulder.)* Jawohl, sit other way.

They both get up and sit down again facing the piano keyboard.

Play you Klavier, Sonya?

SUSCH: For sure, Sonya plays Klavier.

BLATZ: Play you for me, Sonya.

SUSCH: Yoh, why not.

SUSCH reaches out with her forefingers and tentatively plays 'Chopsticks', unaware of the discord caused by beginning on the wrong keys and then the broken, out of tune notes.

BLATZ: Not altogether Beethoven, aber I think with some learning…

BLATZ slips closer to SUSCH and reaches around her from behind and grabs her hands and positions her fingers properly on the keys and they softly play 'Chopsticks' together.

SUSCH: It goes a little bit easier the second time.

BLATZ: Sonya, make not your arms so stiff, let swing with music.

SUSCH: Who anyways is Sonya?

BLATZ: *(As if awakening from a dream.)* What say? Sonya? Sonya plays not piano, Sonya plays violin. Sonya plays violin with angels. Sonya plays…

BLATZ breaks down and cries, clasping Susch tightly as she continues to play 'Chopsticks', slowly building to a crescendo of sound reminiscent of the opening scene.

From the kitchen entrance OBRUM, wearing pants, looks in at SUSCH and BLATZ.

OBRUM: *(Aside.)* What music gives it here?

Music stops. A wisp of hair has shaken loose from Susch's kerchief. SUSCH and BLATZ gaze at each other.

(Aside.) Will I stand by and watch this?

BLATZ reaches out and tucks the hair under the kerchief. BLATZ gazes at SUSCH for a moment, then turns to the piano, and begins to play the opening arpeggios of 'Moonlight Sonata'. SUSCH gazes at BLATZ as she listens to the music.

(*Aside.*) But wait…two years already and nothing. Laughing will not swell my Susch's belly. But funny it would be…

SUSCH: You can sure play a nice song.

BLATZ pauses his playing.

BLATZ: You like it then, the Beethoven.

SUSCH: It is like a spider with long legs.

BLATZ: A spider?

SUSCH: (*Giggles.*) It tickles a little bit. Play again.

BLATZ plays opening arpeggios again until he stumbles on a damaged key. OBRUM approaches the piano.

OBRUM: So my Susch learns to play?

SUSCH: (*Rising from the piano bench.*) Oh, I can't play.

OBRUM: (*Unbuttoning pants.*) I must put on the dress, the itch is still—

SUSCH: Get it yourself.

OBRUM goes into bedroom area and changes into dress. SUSCH kicks the Brummtopp and stomps outside.

BLATZ plays opening of 'Moonlight Sonata' again. OBRUM, adjusting his skirt, approaches BLATZ.

OBRUM: Yes Blatz, learn my Susch to play.

BLATZ ignores OBRUM and plays until he stumbles on a damaged key and he pounds the key in a rage. OBRUM observes him for a moment. He

> *notices the half-hung sheet. He picks up the loose end, steps on the chair and fixes the loop on the hook. Then he tiptoes out.*
>
> *BLATZ continues pounding, then realizing he is alone, stops, rises from the bench, picks up a tool and reaches into the piano.*

BLATZ: Mark that, Sonya, she hears it too. When the music stumbles not, she lets it in. This Klavier I must repair, I must. Aber der Kehler's wife...she is... nein, Sonya, such I must not think.

Scene 6

> *Inside the house. Late at night. The sheet separates BLATZ's piano area from the kitchen and bedroom. BLATZ sits at the piano staring in the direction of the door.*
>
> *SUSCH in her nightdress outside approaches the door.*

SUSCH: *(To herself.)* So late in the field again, and when I ask him what he does, he says, a man must know his land, and then he starts to snore.

> *SUSCH enters kitchen yawning. BLATZ rises from the piano and lies down on his bedding on the floor. SUSCH gazes at the sheet, yawns, turns down the lamp on the table, stretches, casting shadows on the sheet as she does so. She saunters along the sheet to her bed and lies down. SUSCH and BLATZ lie on their sides of the sheet, eyes wide open.*
>
> *OBRUM wearing his skirt lurks in the shadows outside the house. The lamp on the table flickers and goes out.*

Scene 7

December. Winter coats. Farmyard.

OBRUM, wearing dress, and TEEN enter from opposite sides.

OBRUM: Oh Teen, it's good you come.

TEEN: Well, someone must come see what you do with your wife here so far from the village.

OBRUM: A person has to live where he has land to live on.

TEEN: But Obrum, a woman gets lonely and Susch has yet no children. A person would think that way out here with nobody to bother you the snow would be melting.

OBRUM: It itches still, and hurts too when the pants rub.

TEEN: Still? Surely the poison ivy—

OBRUM: Teen, listen, has Susch…did you ever say something to Susch about me?

TEEN: Say what?

OBRUM: You know, about that time…that time I was sick…

TEEN: Why would I say Susch something about that?

OBRUM: Nah well, you and your mother came to help…and you know, Susch has told me that her best friend you are and well…you know.

TEEN: I don't say Susch everything and besides, everything isn't all the time true.

OBRUM: Teen, do you think…could you maybe say something?

TEEN: Obrum, better it would be if you talk to Susch yourself.

OBRUM: But a man can't.

TEEN: Talk about such things?

OBRUM: Please, Teen.

TEEN: Maybe if Susch asks or lets on that she would want to know such a thing, but like I said, everything isn't all the time true.

OBRUM: Bitte Teen, please say her something.

> *OBRUM exits.*

TEEN: What wants that shuzzel now? Was it not enough that I brought Susch and Obrum together when she came to me frightened that her father would yet make her marry Preacher Funk? Before Obrum, Susch was like a three-day drizzle with no sunshine in sight. Is she not now happy?

> *TEEN doesn't notice BLATZ come up behind her.*

TEEN: What wants he yet with this talk of his mumps? And who anyways has poison ivy from thrashing till New Year's? *(Pause.)* Knows not that man—

BLATZ: Nah ja, der Kehler had mumps in boarding school.

TEEN: Oh, you!

BLATZ: Fräulein Schellenberg...ist Fräulein, ja? Nicht Frau? You came with your mother to see Kehler's torment.

TEEN: Speaks he to you too?

BLATZ: Speaks he? You know Kehler, always he speaks double.

TEEN: Yoh, but surely he shleps not our boarding school dummheit talk with him yet?

BLATZ: Nah nah, Schellenberg, dummheit talk in boarding school?

TEEN: Ach you, what do you still here? New Year's Eve it is already.

BLATZ: Die Kunst...das Klavier.

TEEN: Enough with your High Nose German tongue flapping. What do you still here under the feet?

           OBRUM enters still wearing skirt.

OBRUM: Blatz, a word.

           TEEN exits to enter the house.

BLATZ: Jawohl, my friend.

OBRUM: ...December already and the piano is broken still.

BLATZ: Das Klavier ist sensitive. You have instrument obtained that is like...how can I say it...yes like a Stradivarius...found in a garret.

OBRUM: What mean you, Stradivarius?

BLATZ: Eine violin, ja? A fiddle, play strings with bow. In Italy Stradivari made finest violins in the world.

OBRUM: And you say such a thing this piano is?

BLATZ: Aber yes, mein Herr Kehler, such a thing this piano is, only falling the wagon off has something disturbed in the heart.

OBRUM: But three months to make repair? And Susch, learns she to play?

BLATZ: The piano fell a wagon off.

OBRUM: Yes, yoh.

BLATZ: And then too...

OBRUM: Yoh, yes…

BLATZ: The carpenter could be working away building a school in another town.

OBRUM: What mean you?

BLATZ: A woman must have knowing…

OBRUM: Knowing?

BLATZ: Understanding, yes? To learn to play there must be understanding, yes, and wanting also.

OBRUM: Wanting, sure.

BLATZ: And no fear of fault-finding ears when fingers stumble.

OBRUM: Yes, yoh…I think I see. *(Pulls BLATZ close.)* Aber die Susch, she wants…I fear maybe the mumps I had…

BLATZ: Obrum, a carpenter you are, yet like a prince you are patron of my music. I must go…the instrument waits.

OBRUM: *(Holding on.)* Blatz, I shall see about winter work. But a patron, wish you my meaning to grasp, will want to come home to a tuned instrument.

BLATZ: *(Laughing.)* Mein prince jawohl, ich bin Herr Doktor Tuning Fork.

            OBRUM exits.

Ach Sonya, have I no soul that I pursue this foolish music dream when you…are no more? And yet, the music will not die. Almost had I pushed it from my soul, but then this peasant Kehler obtains a Klavier to tempt me. *(Sound of Model T driving off.)* And dwelling near this peasant woman my longing for you and our music washes over me…like our late night improvisations in Ekaterinoslav.

SUSCH and TEEN enter carrying clothes basket. SUSCH is wearing clothespin apron.

SUSCH: Blatz, don't lie yet on the bed. The sheets first must dry.

TEEN: Freeze stiff they will first.

BLATZ: Die Kunst…das Klavier…I must repair.

BLATZ exits.

TEEN helps SUSCH hang wash during the conversation.

SUSCH: *(Sighs.)* Sometimes I feel like I am a corner growing full with spider webs.

TEEN: But Susch, with a man in the house spider webs shouldn't be growing in the corners.

SUSCH: What you mean? *(Understands.)* Oh you…just wait, when you get married you'll see that so simple it isn't!

TEEN: But for sure Obrum knows what to do?

SUSCH: Oh ganz gewiss he knows, but…

TEEN: You mean Obrum can't?

SUSCH: Oh Obrum can, and he has too.

TEEN: So what's loose then? You don't like to?

SUSCH: Oh, I like…but…oh Teen, before the wedding, Preacher Funk came to the garden…almost dark it was and he said that Obrum couldn't…and for sure I told Preacher Funk off good because I knew for sure that Obrum could and he had…only then a few days after the wedding it all was nothing… and now over two years and nothing again. Could it be true what Funk said?

TEEN: Such a thing isn't all the time true. Believe me Susch. But yeah…*(Pause.)*

SUSCH: Tell me.

TEEN: Uh, well…the winter before Obrum's parents moved away to Mexico Obrum had mumps. He was twenty and the mumps went down and, yoh, my mother went to help him and she saw how bad it was. But Susch believe me, such a thing isn't all the time true. Mother knows at least half a dozen men who had mumps that went down to the balls and still they have children.

SUSCH: Is that so?

TEEN: Only some whisper about a Gypsy in the hayloft.

SUSCH: Oh but Teen, people wouldn't.

TEEN: Tongues will always flap.

SUSCH: Teen, I think so with Obrum it's true…

TEEN: Oh Susch, just try again.

SUSCH: It's not so easy when…

TEEN: When what?

SUSCH: My heart clappers when he is close.

TEEN: What mean you?

SUSCH: Even now when we have lived already two years together…

TEEN: Oh.

SUSCH: …sometimes we are so close that I can believe we really are one flesh and then another time so far apart we are that Obrum could be on the moon. Is it because we are still alone? Just we two?

Sound of piano.

But no...never just we two...not just Obrum and me...no, it is only always me alone with that Mensch who calls me Sonya. Only always, "Bitte Sonya, hear once you this, hear once you this," and he plays that plaguing music over and over until something irks him and he stops and hammers and clangs on those thousand wires in that piano until my head aches. How can we reach for each other in the night when we know Blatz with his ears listens on the other side of the curtain? Ah, but then, sometimes the piano stays fixed up long enough so Blatz can play his song all the way through without stopping. And then I want to smile and cry at the same time, so pretty it is, like a mourning dove cooing back to a person. And if he plays when I am kneading bread, my soul rises up past the moon all the way to the stars. My backbones shiver and I think I should just let him call me Sonya already and I feel again how he reached out and pushed my hair back under my kerchief and I can't bear that Sonya woman he was touching in his heart...

TEEN: Holem de gruel

SUSCH: ...and then...for an eyeblink the piano playing fills me like a child. Oh Teen could it be...am I...the unfruitful one?

TEEN: Oh no Susch! *(Embraces SUSCH.)* Lord knows, I would father you a child myself, if only God had given me the means.

SUSCH: *(Aside, as she shrugs out of embrace.)* You wear a dress too. *(To Teen.)* Oh look, it snows.

TEEN: And windy too. I must go before it is altogether dark.

SUSCH: Where is the Model T?

TEEN:	Obrum is gone?
SUSCH:	Gone on New Year's Eve? Gott im Himmel, how can a person try again when her man is away? I have no Gypsy in the hayloft, only a Klaviermensch who says, 'Hear once you this'.

SUSCH exits.

TEEN:	Huy yuy yuy. Have I set the lamp too near the straw?

TEEN exits.

Scene 8

Piano room. Kitchen.

BLATZ plays opening bars of 'Moonlight Sonata', stopping and starting again, playing a few bars further, stopping and starting again. BLATZ's playing stumbles on an out-of-tune key. BLATZ hammers at the faulty key and weeps.

BLATZ:	Ach Sonya, I stumble over Beethoven's notes and yet I dream the lie that music worthy of a human ear I can play. Oh to be deaf, like the master himself. What said that English poet? "Heard melodies are sweet, but those unheard are sweeter." Aber yet when the melodies heard are not sweet I fear that the melodies unheard will so hellish be... and yet Sonya, when I touch the keys of this broken instrument, now and then I can feel with my soul's ear the drawing of your bow across the strings of your Gypsy violin, improvising on my poor Beethoven and I believe the lie and I think, if only your scherzos I could hear, if only your teasing touch I could feel yet again, then I could composition make with this hellish mess of notes that torments me.

BLATZ rises from the piano, enters the kitchen and warms himself by the stove. He looks around for SUSCH. He hears the wind outside. He looks out the window.

To town, Kehler said. And a storm also. Why mutters he about mumps to Teen? Talks he dummheit when he speaks of returning to a tuned instrument? Surely he means not...my patron he is... but wish I his meaning to grasp? No matter, betrayal there will be...ach meine Susch, Sonya lives when you are near. Your peasant home is my conservatory...my refuge from the dreadful school.

BLATZ moves back to the piano.

Oh Sonya, lass ich die Muzik sterben...let I the music die, would not I then betray you?

BLATZ pounds the opening chord of 'Moonlight Sonata', as if trying to correct the instrument through force. BLATZ plays the chord again, gently this time.

SUSCH enters, sets milk pails down beside separator, takes off her barn coat as she listens to BLATZ play on, weeping audibly along with the music. She starts toward Blatz's room, but pauses at the Brummtopp and unconsciously runs her finger through the swatch of horse hair.

SUSCH: Still the dress and the poison ivy...and now he has left me alone with this.

Howling wind. The house shakes. The lamp flickers. SUSCH clasps her arms against the chill. During the folloowing exchange SUSCH moves about the house, slowly "circling" closer to BLATZ, until she turns down the lamp and joins BLATZ on the piano bench.

Know you where my man went?

BLATZ stops playing.

BLATZ: He talked of town to see about carpenter work.

SUSCH: On New Year's Eve?

BLATZ: I thought not that today he would go. A person could smell that storming would soon come.

SUSCH: Where can he stay for night in town?

BLATZ: Kehler knows people.

SUSCH: At least then he isn't stuck someplace in the snow.

BLATZ: Ja, at least not that.

          Sounds of the wind, creaking house.

SUSCH: Tell me…about piano…how did you learn?

          Gust of wind flickers the lamp. BLATZ hunches down on the piano bench as if the weight of the world is on his shoulders.

BLATZ: Der Schul Lehrer Herr Sawatsky was musician. Klavier he had in the village school, and when he found awareness of my curiosity for music, lessons he gave me after school even if my parents had not money to pay him.

          Sawatsky showed me also how to fix small errors in tuning on a piano and one day he sent me to my landlord's house to tune the Middle C octave. Sawatsky mumbled that the landlord's daughter was tone deaf, but would maybe be nice to hold like cello.

SUSCH: Cello? What mean you?

BLATZ: Oh ja, cello ist eine grosse violin—a big fiddle, ja, and for playing, the musician holds it between his knees, one hand on the neck and the other hand saws strings with bow.

SUSCH: And your Sawatsky wanted to hold the girl like that?

BLATZ: Nah ja, der Sawatsky was sometimes a Schweinkopf and...

SUSCH: But Sonya, she was this daughter?

BLATZ: Aber nein, never could a Sonya have come from such a village.

SUSCH: How come not?

BLATZ: Die Luft...hard to breathe it was...after I met Sonya the village felt choked off with spider webs...

SUSCH: But this Sonya was like a cello that you wanted between your knees to hold?

> *A gust of wind shudders the house. SUSCH turns down the lamp. The scene continues in darkness. Opening movement of 'Moonlight Sonata' plays softly then is joined by a violin improvising playfully, mischievously on BLATZ's theme.*

> *SUSCH joins BLATZ on the piano bench.*

BLATZ: Sonya, nein, someone will yet come. The storm...

> *SUSCH embraces BLATZ's arm, leans her head on his shoulder.*

SUSCH: For the last time, Blatz, my name is Susch, and who will come in such a storm?

> *BLATZ leans his head, raises his other arm.*

BLATZ: A sonata I will compose to you.

SUSCH: Sonata? Plays she fiddle too?

BLATZ: First an adagio sostenuto, a hymn to Christ on moonlight water walking.

SUSCH: I thought it was daytime when he did that.

BLATZ: I know the moonlight came after, and the blind girl...

SUSCH: Now a blind girl yet? How many have you...

BLATZ: Beethoven and his friend walking in the night heard a harpsichord from a lowly house on a poor street. The music was of Beethoven's own composing. When they knocked, the door opened, and a shoemaker told them that his blind sister was the player. The sister had learned the music by listening outside the open window of a rich house.

SUSCH: So if I listen to you play I could learn?

SUSCH throws her arms around BLATZ.

BLATZ: And the brother asked if Beethoven would play for his blind sister, even on such a poor instrument.

SUSCH: Was it broken too?

BLATZ: No, but the poor people's last candle burned out.

SUSCH: Like by us?

BLATZ: And Beethoven's friend opened the window shutters and moonlight streamed over the poor woman's instrument.

SUSCH: In a snowstorm it wouldn't work so good.

BLATZ takes SUSCH's hand.

BLATZ: And Beethoven said, "I shall compose a sonata to the moonlight."

SUSCH: Had he such long fingers yet too?

BLATZ: The opening movement...a whispered breathing, a bridge from the stifling village to the minuet of the allegretto dancing into presto agitato—the thunderstorm.

SUSCH: Gives it thunder with a snowstorm?

> *BLATZ embraces SUSCH in a Clark Gable-Vivien Leigh pose. As he speaks the next lines he lifts her to her feet and walks her around the floor in an awkward, yet lovely dance.*

BLATZ: And Sonya, you said, "Always Blatz with that hundred-year-old German music. When will you open your ears to the twentieth century? Play some Rachmaninoff, Prokofiev, Shostakovich, yes, Shostakovich!"

SUSCH: Shostakovich? Is that a woman too?

> *BLATZ and SUSCH fumble with each other's clothes as they dance.*

BLATZ: And I said, "Aber der Beethoven is a genius. Sonata 14, a bridge from classic to romantic. Two traditions in one composition. Sonata quasi una fantasia!"

SUSCH: Are you now yet a Catholic?

BLATZ: And Sonya said, "Ah yes, my dear Beethoven Blatz, the German genius moved forward with his times. No slave to Mozart or Haydn he was. He took up the spirit of Napoleon and shrugged off stifling tradition." And I said to her, "Aber meine liebe Sonya, you cannot mean Mozart or Haydn could ever stifling be!" and Sonya said, "Oh yes, my lovely man who would Beethoven be, oh yes, even Mozart stifles when turned into a god."

> *BLATZ and SUSCH stumble onto the piano bench. They squirm and fumble as they talk so that they find the "cello position".*

SUSCH: Here let me help you.

BLATZ: "Bitte wait!" I cried.

SUSCH: I waited already two years.

> *Outside TEEN stumbles through the storm toward the dark house. She is carrying a package.*

BLATZ: "Played as it should be Sonata 14 is as revolutionary as any young Russian, yet Beethoven forgets not the sonorous nature of love."

SUSCH: Sonorous, sonata, Sonya. But I am Susch!

> *TEEN appears to hear SUSCH's cry, and stops before she reaches the door.*

BLATZ: Still Sonya argued, "But Blatz, mein lieber Herr, the adagio sostenuto is not a love song, it is a funeral hymn by a genius who desired love but feared it more."

SUSCH: Blatz, mein lieber Herr, I am with you here. You can talk to me.

BLATZ: Sonya, bitte hear once you this.

> *SUSCH is riding BLATZ in "cello position".*

SUSCH: Is this how a man holds a cello?

BLATZ: Aber bitte Susch, hear once you this.

SUSCH: Now yet he calls me Susch and I hear only my clappering heart.

BLATZ: Sonya I hear it. Das Klavier, it waits for my new notes.

> *BLATZ slips out from under SUSCH.*

SUSCH: (*Rising from bench.*) No, wait, I think not the sonata is altogether come to the end.

> *BLATZ opens piano bench, rummages around and pulls out a sheaf of papers.*

(Moving to kitchen.) Obrum at least snores for a while after he…oh…

SUSCH lights lamp.

Gott im Himmel, have I done this? Hungers a woman so much that she will reach where she should not reach? *(Faint sounds of piano.)* What? Now he plays piano? What kind of Mensch? *(Laughs.)* Teen you said a Gypsy in the hayloft. *(Laughs.)* Could it be a Klaviermensch too? *(Laughs.)* Obrum, you said a rainbow in the sky. *(Laughs.)* Obrum, you would see a rainbow in a snowstorm? *(Laughs.)* Obrum, you would maybe laugh? *(Laugh cut off by sound of a gust of wind. She shivers.)* Will it… will it one time be enough?

Howling wind. Knocking. Piano stops.

TEEN enters. She carries the package.

SUSCH: Teen! What do you here?

TEEN: The snow, I couldn't see, I got lost…

SUSCH: How did you find here?

TEEN: The wind…I walked away from the wind…and then chimney smoke I could smell.

SUSCH: You could smell smoke in the storm?

TEEN: Yes, and then when I could see little bit light from your house I got hooked on the washline.

SUSCH: Obrum went to town.

TEEN: Yes, I…in this storm?

SUSCH: He stays by people he knows in town.

TEEN: Oh. That's good then that I came so you won't be— *(Piano playing resumes.)* Alone you aren't.

SUSCH: No. Come sit by the stove. You must be chilled through.

> *TEEN sits at table near stove. SUSCH adds wood to the fire.*

(Yawns.) A storm always makes me tired.

> *BLATZ plays the same run of notes over and over.*

TEEN: Bothers you not that tiresome noise?

SUSCH: A person can get used to it...like a man's snoring.

TEEN: Such a thing I couldn't stand.

SUSCH: But bothersome it is when...sleep will not come.

TEEN: You mean he makes such noise in the night?

SUSCH: Not so loud, just so a little bit I can hear...just enough. *(Yawns.)*

TEEN: Shall I tell Blatz already to be still?

SUSCH: No, he will soon be still. *(Yawns.)* He is a Mensch too, even if he doesn't *(Yawns.)* snore like Obrum.

TEEN: Oh.

SUSCH: When everything is still I get up from the bed and open Blatz's curtain so the stove can heat his room too. *(Yawns.)* Come Teen, let's to bed before we get so sleepy we fall out of the chair.

> *SUSCH and TEEN go to bed. BLATZ plays fade out notes.*

Scene 9

Next day. Kitchen. Stove. Bedroom.

BLATZ carries an ink bottle from his piano room and warms it over the stove. He holds a straight pen in his other hand.

TEEN and SUSCH in the bedroom. TEEN hands SUSCH the package.

SUSCH: What mean you with this?

SUSCH opens the package and pulls out a fancy red dress.

TEEN: Ach Susch, a woman can't always just have on a milking dress.

SUSCH: What matters it, here in this cold grain shed house?

TEEN: You looked so beautiful by the wedding.

SUSCH: I ran the whole way, I was so excited…and scared too and then I fell down in the creek.

TEEN: Yes, you were mud all the way to your head.

SUSCH: And I was scared how I could get married when my dress was dripping wet.

TEEN: But Obrum had brought a wedding dress.

SUSCH: Yes, Obrum always brings me things…

TEEN: Come, try it on.

SUSCH: Ach you, I don't think I should.

TEEN: It will make you feel like your wedding day.

SUSCH: Maybe…

BLATZ sits at the kitchen table and draws lines (staves) on sheets of paper.

Oh look, such lace.

TEEN: For you, lace yes.

TEEN: (*Helps SUSCH into the fancy dress.*) Arms up…see, it
             falls down nice…let me hook it closed.

SUSCH: So now what?

TEEN: Go once into the kitchen so you have room to turn
             around.

> *SUSCH enters the kitchen wearing the fancy red
> dress. She hesitates when she sees BLATZ, then with
> determination she steps up to the stove to warm her
> hands. BLATZ rises from the table with his pen in
> his hand.*

BLATZ: Sonya!

SUSCH: (*Whispers.*) What, Mensch, still you cannot see me?

BLATZ: Hear once you this!

SUSCH: Not again!

> *Their eyes lock. BLATZ moves his pen as if he is
> writing in the air with it. His head nods as if he
> is hearing music in his head. SUSCH follows the
> moving pen with her eyes and starts to nod her head
> in time to music she hears in her head too. Then
> SUSCH laughs.*

> *TEEN enters the kitchen unobserved and watches
> SUSCH and BLATZ in their mental embrace.*

> *OBRUM enters, now wearing new trousers, pauses
> unnoticed, then stomps his snowy boots across the
> floor.*

OBRUM: The bridegroom is come back!

> *He grabs SUSCH and shrubbers her with his two-*

day beard and then he kisses her so hard that it looks like he will devour her.

BLATZ flees to the piano and starts to pound out the presto agitato (3rd) movement of 'Moonlight Sonata', until some notes sound off key. Then BLATZ hammers at a single chord as if trying to destroy the instrument. OBRUM stops kissing.

What's loose with him?

SUSCH shrugs herself out from his arms. OBRUM sees TEEN putting on her coat.

Teen what do you here anyways?

TEEN: Somebody has to stay with your wife in a storm.

OBRUM: The whole night you were here?

SUSCH: She slept with me in our bed.

OBRUM: In our bed Teen slept?

SUSCH: And she doesn't snore neither.

OBRUM: Always you come, Teen.

SUSCH: It was good that you came.

TEEN: What a man can't, a woman must. *(She sneaks a glare at OBRUM.)*

            TEEN exits.

            OBRUM pulls off his coat and hangs it on the nail by the door. He sits down on the little bench by the door and pulls off his boots.

OBRUM: Susch, I will build us a new house.

SUSCH: Where were you for night?

OBRUM: Gretna and it stormed so bad that I had to stay.

SUSCH:	Why didn't you say me something? I went to milk the cows and the Model T was gone. And then it started to blow and snow and you weren't home and I didn't know where you could be and I was alone.
OBRUM:	Blatz was here with you, not?
SUSCH:	But he isn't my man.

SUSCH begins to cry.

OBRUM:	Nah sure, he isn't your man. (*OBRUM puts his arms around her belly and shrubbers her neck with his whiskers.*) I'm your man, Susch. Don't you believe me that?
SUSCH:	Let me cook already. I'm hungry, too.

OBRUM lets her go.

OBRUM:	Ach Mensch, I didn't bring in the stuff from Gretna.
SUSCH:	You mean you brought the new house in the car?

OBRUM hurries on his coat and steps into his boots.

OBRUM:	That dress fits you good!
SUSCH:	Shuft!

OBRUM laughs as he exits.

SUSCH starts to pull off the fancy dress as she steps toward the bedroom, then turns to look at the door.

Wears he again pants?

SUSCH goes into the bedroom area.

BLATZ starts playing softly.

> *OBRUM enters and sets a rocking chair with a red bow tied around it in the middle of the floor.*

> *SUSCH enters, pulling her fancy red dress into place as if she has taken it off, changed her mind, and put it back on again.*

> *SUSCH notices rocking chair.*

Who is that for?

OBRUM: For you to rock the baby.

SUSCH: You brought a baby from Gretna, too?

OBRUM: No, but you will have a baby and then you will need this rocking chair.

SUSCH: How is a woman anyways supposed to have a baby if her man is away in Gretna for night?

> *OBRUM grabs SUSCH around the waist again.*

OBRUM: Oh but girl, God made days, too!

SUSCH: Ach du Blatz.

> *OBRUM drags SUSCH off to the shadowy bedroom.*

> *BLATZ stands at piano writing on his manuscript paper on top of the piano. He stops from time to time to listen to the lovemaking. The audience will see shadowy lovemaking movements, though the passion of the scene is carried by the dialogue.*

What want you with your hand?

OBRUM: Ah Susch, I just want to be you good.

SUSCH: So dringent, Obrum, so dringent…

OBRUM: Ah Susch, I am your man, believe me that!

SUSCH: I believe you that. So lostijch, so dringent.

OBRUM: Ach Susch, such schmausing, such lostijchkeit.

SUSCH: I waited so long for your Menschlijchkeit, so long.

OBRUM: Susch, never wait. Just reach for it.

SUSCH: Ach Jung, the window frost will yet melt.

OBRUM: Then the moon can shine clearer through.

SUSCH: Holy smokes, will the bed hold?

OBRUM: I am you so good, I am you so good.

SUSCH: Huy, yuy yuy!

OBRUM: Dusent noch emol eent!

SUSCH: Will you live? You are puffing like an old dog.

OBRUM: A man who will be a father must live.

SUSCH: *(Yawning.)* A father would be good.

OBRUM: *(Yawning.)* What you mean?

SUSCH: Nothing, here let me shrug out from under you. Even a lostijch little man gets weighty on the breast.

OBRUM: Put your head here.

SUSCH: Your heart clappers so hard.

OBRUM: Ach yoh, liebe Susch, it clappers for you.

           BLATZ plays. Barely audible. Tentative. BLATZ is furtively trying out his new composition.

SUSCH: Hear you that? He has not played that music before.

OBRUM: *(Drowsily.)* What say you?

SUSCH: How long yet will that Blatz stay here?

OBRUM: *(Fading out.)* I think so the piano is fixed almost.

             BLATZ hits an out-of-tune key.

SUSCH: I will try to believe you that.

             Snoring joins the soft piano playing. Blatz stops to write notes on paper. Plays again.

BLATZ: Ach liebe Sonya, you told me right. Music must rouse the flesh, music must erupt from the loins—ah Sonya, what music our love and lust could have made had the anarchists not…Sonya, I flounder in despair…but no, the anarchists must not win. This peasant woman is the angel sent by you, Sonya, to set free unheard melodies. *(TEEN, wearing a gaudy mask and dressed in man's Gypsy clothing, slinks in to the Brummtopp.)* To shrug off this gift would deny you, Sonya. But I must have caution…I must keep up my welcome here. Pray that my unwitting patron decides not too soon that my task is done.

             TEEN dips her hands in the water basin, grasps the horse hair swatch, and begins to rub it between her fingers, creating a rummeling sound.

             Gott im Himmel! Das Anarchie kommt wieder!

             SUSCH, her red dress disheveled, steps into the kitchen light.

SUSCH: I am just a woman…I want not much!

             TEEN develops a rhythm fitting the song.

TEEN: *(Sings to the tune of "Ode to Joy")*

             Wish the husband a great harvest
             As this new year is begun
             Wish the wife a brilliant red dress
             May she also bear a son.

             Wish the house guest inspiration

> May he take his muse and go
> Where his notes ring o'er creation
> Covering fears with drifting snow

OBRUM: Will Blatz have something to tell me?

TEEN: *(Sings.)* Cover it o'er with drifting snow.

Blackout.

Act II

Scene 1

Winter. A few days later.

Kitchen.

SUSCH dozes in rocking chair.

Outdoors.

OBRUM and BLATZ enter.

BLATZ: Mein lieber Kehler, the music rumbles around in my head like a thunderstorm on the steppe with rainbows shining through rain.

OBRUM: In the winter?

BLATZ: Orchestras my head hears, the winds, the brass, the strings, the timpani…ah, to squeeze all these notes from the keys of this Klavier you have before me set.

BLATZ grabs OBRUM by the shoulders.

Forever in your debt I shall be. Even Meister Ludwig van Beethoven had not such a patron. No prince could provide me such an instrument.

OBRUM extricates himself from BLATZ's grasp.

OBRUM: Then the piano is fixed? It is in tune?

BLATZ: In tune? Fixed? Such a Klavier is delicate and temperamental like great music itself. Soothed it

must be, tightened and loosened, hammered and
tickled, gespielt mit schwunk. Only then will it
yield up the sonatas hidden therein.

OBRUM: So the repair is not completed?

BLATZ: Such an instrument cannot be hastened, it is not a
milk cow.

OBRUM: Blatz, listen! Have you...did you...achieve
harmony in the storm?

BLATZ: Sturm und Drang, mein lieber Kehler, such was for
Goethe and Beethoven. We are in a new world. Look
out over your virgin steppe. Pastoral melodies lie
in wait under that snow. With your kind patronage
those melodies I shall compose.

OBRUM: Maybe then a new piano we need. How can Susch
learn if the piano stays not in tune?

BLATZ: Aber nein, my generous Patron, the faults in the
Klavier are its genius, like the deafness of great
Beethoven.

OBRUM: If such a wonderful instrument this piano is I
should haul it to Schanzenfeld where I hear a new
teacher they need.

BLATZ grabs OBRUM by the shoulders.

BLATZ: Hear once you this, Kehler. Your sweet peasant wife
will yet learn.

OBRUM shoves BLATZ away.

OBRUM: Tuned instrument or not, piano learning must
begin.

BLATZ: I shall yet please you, my kind patron, but you
must let me have time. As you well know, to play
harmonies the players must agree on the melody.
Ah, but I must walk and listen to the notes in the
cold air.

BLATZ exits.

OBRUM: Understood he my meaning? And would my Susch so hasty to the melody agree? With Teen yet staying for night? Dummkopp I am for sure. I must first lead my Susch into the melody.

OBRUM exits.

Kitchen.

SUSCH stirs in rocking chair, then opens her eyes.

SUSCH: How knew he my weakness in thinking that stormy night? What else yet hears a man who hears music in his head? Oh let it hold...Gott im Himmel, just let it hold...the piano will be fixed up and Blatz will be gone away and Obrum will build a house that's not so cold!

SUSCH rises as if to add wood to the stove, but her eye is drawn to BLATZ's curtain. She tiptoes into BLATZ's room. Piano. Sheet music. Ink bottle. Pen. Piano bench. Bed on floor. Box.

No loose pieces lying around that I can see. *(Her hand brushes her stomach unconsciously.)* He can go. *(Touches a key.)* But who would play piano then? Not Obrum, for sure not me. *(She notices the sheet music on the music rack.)* But what has that man here? *(Reads.)* 'Klavieren... Son...ata Nummer Eins für Sonya'...but then he has the 'Sonya' crossed out and beside it he writes 'Susch'. Klavieren Sonata Nummer Eins für Susch. And then he draws lines with balls and sticks all over them. I think I feel a bit dizzy. But what quotes here? *(Reads.)* 'Forgive it me Sonya, aber this simple peasant woman comforts and stirs me still.'

SUSCH shuffles through the pages.

Oh? Such a simple woman I am not!

SUSCH crumples the pages one by one, then gathers the balls of paper up in her arms. One ball drops to the floor without her noticing. She carries them to the kitchen. She lifts the cover off the stove and stares at the flames for a moment, then drops the pages in.

Now Blatz will go!

SUSCH puts on her clothespin apron, picks up laundry basket and as she exits, she has to squeeze past BLATZ as he enters. SUSCH avoids looking at him, but BLATZ turns to watch her set down her basket at the washline. OBRUM joins SUSCH and helps her take down the laundry and fold it for the basket. Inaudible conversation.

BLATZ conducts an invisible orchestra as he turns away from the lovely domestic scene outdoors and moves into his piano room where he sees balled up manuscript page, picks it up and smooths it out at the piano. He stares intently at the page for a moment, then balls it up again and sets it on the piano.

BLATZ: What a gift from the muse! To have certain disaster ripped from one's cowardly grasp. Oh woman you cannot know that you have done what I had not courage to do.

He picks up blank paper and quickly sketches a staff with a straight pen.

Anew I can begin, unburdened by my clumsy scribbles.

He writes, humming softly. He pauses, raises the pen, and conducts an orchestra. He writes, then picks up the paper and paces about the room, his head nodding in time to inner music. Then he sits down at the piano, places the sheet on the music rack.

Hear once you this. *(Plays a few notes.)* Gut, gut.

(Plays more notes.) Nein, nein. *(Plays same notes again.)* Nein. *(Writes on sheet.)* Ja, better. *(Plays revised notes.)* Nein, nein. *(Pounds an out-of-tune key. Thinks. Writes on the paper. Plays a chord that works with the out-of-tune key.)* Aber ja, Sonya, this devil can yet succeed. *(Plays the chord again.)* I need the peasant woman again. Means he not that? Why she destroyed my clumsy pages I know not, but… *(Plays a variation of the chord.)* the muse, I must not let it fade. My unwitting muse. *(Writes more notes. Plays a new chord and then adds a trill.)* Aha, even a thought can feed the music. Ah Sonya, this humble conservatory I must not leave. Ach, such a patron. This instrument my deafness shall be. But always back to the starting place I must go. Diese Frau ist die Quelle!

> *BLATZ plays opening movement of 'Moonlight Sonata'. Playing continues as background through next scene.*

> *Outside. Clothesline.*

> *OBRUM and SUSCH taking down wash.*

SUSCH: Ach du, such a thing people wouldn't do. Anyways who sees gypsies around here?

OBRUM: People do what they have to do.

SUSCH: But such a thing would stay in a person's head, not?

OBRUM: Well maybe yes, but if people get what they need, if what they get is good, then maybe it doesn't need to bother a person's head.

SUSCH: Anyways, such a thing I couldn't do.

OBRUM: Well no…but if a time comes when you get hartsoft dringent for something…

SUSCH picks up the filled basket and nudges him with her hip.

SUSCH: Dringent like you get in the bed?

OBRUM: Well yoh, dringent like that.

SUSCH: With a man as dringent as you a woman would never get dringent as that!

OBRUM embraces SUSCH.

OBRUM: This man is dringent now.

OBRUM kisses SUSCH.

SUSCH: Obrum, ach du...I must take the wash in.

BLATZ stops playing, opens up balled up manuscript page, balls it up again and stares deep in thought.

OBRUM carries basket into house. SUSCH follows.

OBRUM: Soon I will build a room where you can wash clothes.

SUSCH: With a washing machine too?

OBRUM: Oh for sure, everything the best for Susch.

SUSCH: And where will you get money to pay for all this?

OBRUM: Susch, I have paid for wood in Gretna to bring home when the snow is gone. Besides, Ritz builds a new elevator and I have hired on with him.

SUSCH: You're leaving me here all alone?

OBRUM: Blatz will be here.

SUSCH: What? You would leave a woman who is...*(She revises her sentence.)* you would leave me alone with Blatz?

OBRUM: Well sure, what's loose with that?

SUSCH: I thought he would already go, the piano is put together.

OBRUM: But it is not in tune. The music needs a tuned instrument. You like the music, not?

                SUSCH turns her back on OBRUM.

SUSCH: Well, I have to feed the dog anyways.

                OBRUM grabs SUSCH and swings her around in a wild embrace.

OBRUM: Susch, liebe Susch, believe me, I am your man.

SUSCH: Put me down, let me go.

                OBRUM gently settles her into the rocking chair.

OBRUM: Oh but yes, you will have a baby soon.

SUSCH: How know...yes, yes, a baby for my Obrum. *(Laughs.)* God help me have a baby for my Obrum.

OBRUM: Nah sure, God will help and I *(Kisses her.)* will milk the cows for you today.

                OBRUM picks up the milk pails and exits.

SUSCH: What wants he from me now? And why talks he about what some people do to get what they want? What if he knows—

                BLATZ rises from piano, balled up manuscript page in hand. Pretending not to notice SUSCH's presence, BLATZ tosses the balled up manuscript page in the air and catches it. Then he walks over to the stove and drops it into the flames. He turns, pretending surprise to see SUSCH in the rocking chair.

                Oh, I—

BLATZ: Say nothing, dear woman.

BLATZ grabs SUSCH's hand and pulls her up from the rocking chair into an embrace.

SUSCH: No, what do you? Obrum—

SUSCH struggles against his embrace, but BLATZ holds on.

BLATZ: Susch, Susch, your burning, ja, your burning feeds the fire of my music.

BLATZ lowers SUSCH back into the rocking chair and sets her rocking. He turns to go to the piano, then stops as if remembering something, turns back to SUSCH and grabs her hand and pulls her up.

Come liebchen, der Kehler wishes for you to learn Klavierspiel. We must obey the patron.

BLATZ pulls her over to the piano.

SUSCH: Mensch, have we not done enough?

BLATZ: Nein, nein, der Kehler wishes it. He wishes a musical wife to have.

BLATZ settles SUSCH on the piano bench and sits beside her.

First we find Mittel C. *(Plays Middle C.)* Then we can play a tone ladder. *(Plays scale.)* Now you play.

SUSCH: If you say Kehler wishes it. *(Plays scale with one finger but includes black keys as well.)*

BLATZ: Nein, nein, not yet the schwartze keys. Hear once you this.

BLATZ plays the scale up and down, but then seems to forget SUSCH's lesson and plays a bar of his new composition. SUSCH watches in awe as he plays on, then she slips away from the piano bench.

SUSCH: *(Whisper.)* Fire could burn a piano, not. Would he go
                 then? *(Listens to another bar of BLATZ's music, which
                 then stops. She stares at BLATZ, listening to the silence.)*
                 What place goes he? Where goes he first to hear
                 the music that he plays? *(Silence continues.)* How
                 come it is…that I want to go to that place with him?
                 (SUSCH places her hand on her belly.) It must be…oh
                 let it just hold.

Scene 2

                 Spring. Outdoors. Kitchen. Piano room.

                 *BLATZ playing piano quietly. TEEN and SUSCH
                 outside approaching the house. Spring sounds.*

TEEN: And the creek is full so I had to go around by the
                 high bridge.

SUSCH: Yes, too deep even for high boots.

TEEN: And that water is ice cold.

                 *BLATZ stops playing. He picks his notebook and
                 pen and steps outside.*

BLATZ: Ah, die Luft. It stifles not. A man must walk the
                 steppe and listen. *(Looks at SUSCH.)* Das Klavier
                 waits.

                 BLATZ bows slightly to TEEN and exits.

TEEN: What means he?

                 SUSCH and TEEN enter the house.

SUSCH: Obrum wants I should learn piano.

TEEN: And he leaves you alone to learn?

                 *SUSCH moves to the piano, sits down. TEEN
                 follows.*

SUSCH: Oh no, just practice I do alone, when he is not making new sonata. Learning we do together. He sits me beside and shows me how to play.

TEEN: *(Sits on bench beside SUSCH.)* Show me then.

SUSCH: For sure. *(Showing off, plays the C scale up and down, barely stumbling.)*

TEEN: Who would have thought.

SUSCH: No, that's not my music. That's what he wants me to play, but when he is not here, I play this. *(Plays 'Chopsticks'.)*

TEEN: That I can play too.

SUSCH: You can?

> *TEEN plays 'Chopsticks'.*

SUSCH: Obrum showed me that. We played it together.

TEEN: Let's try together then.

SUSCH: OK.

> *They play together until they stumble and burst out laughing and embrace each other.*

TEEN: Oh Susch, it is good you laugh.

> *SUSCH slips out of the embrace and plays a few notes of 'Chopsticks'.*

SUSCH: Such a plague this noise, like a buggy spring squeaking from church all the way home. *(Tries to play an arpeggio.)* Even that is just a plaguing noise, hollow like a dried-out earth cherry husk.

TEEN: What mean you?

SUSCH: But when Blatz's fingers crawl over this piano like a long-legged spider it is like that earth cherry grows back, and I can taste it, yellow and ripe, not sweet, not sour, I can taste it in...in hidden places...

TEEN: Oh but Susch.

SUSCH: When he plays that Moonlight song, and that new song, that Sonya thing he writes on this paper here...ach no, still he calls me Sonya. Gott im Himmel, what yet is my wanting?

TEEN: Huy, yuy, yuy!

SUSCH: Oh Teen, can you feel such a thing?

TEEN: Me?

SUSCH turns from the piano and rummages through a wooden apple crate.

SUSCH: Look what he does here. (*Holds up music manuscript.*) Music writing...Sonya sonata...Susch sonata... make your mind up Blatz, you can't anyways have two...only sometimes...what is this here? Pages enough to make a Bible. If I had burned this too... and what sticks out here? A picture...a woman... young, a fiddle...like a baby in her arms.

TEEN: 'Liebe Sonya' it says on the back.

SUSCH: Sees he yet something of her when he looks at me?

TEEN: Such a nose you don't have.

SUSCH: And for sure not earrings bommeling down like drips from a nose.

TEEN: And such eyebrows. Fah, I think that Blatz is going blind.

SUSCH: You think so?

SUSCH tucks the picture into her apron pocket.

BLATZ enters.

TEEN: Oh.

SUSCH seats herself at the piano. TEEN moves into the kitchen. BLATZ bows slightly and steps past her to the piano. BLATZ seats himself beside SUSCH.

BLATZ: Nah ja, play me what you have learned.

SUSCH plays the C scale in a plodding manner. TEEN watches, slowly backing up to sit in the rocking chair.

Better a little bit, aber the wrist…too stiff, ja. Let fingers step from key to key, like walking barefoot on soft grass. Here *(He puts his arm around her to reach the keys.)* start with this finger, then this one, and then this one. *(Demonstrates.)*

SUSCH tries, almost plays through, but stumbles on the last note.

SUSCH: Ach, my ears can hear it but my fingers won't listen.

BLATZ: Here, let's together play something.

SUSCH: Chopsticks?

BLATZ: No, too fine your ears are for 'Chopsticks'. Give me your fingers.

BLATZ guides her hand to the keys for the opening two-fingered bass chord of the 'Moonlight Sonata.'

Play that. Just two fingers see. *(SUSCH plays chord.)* Again. *(She plays.)* Again. *(She plays.)* Good, now move fingers down one key. Play. *(She plays.)* Again. *(She plays.)* Again. *(She plays.)* Now play the first one. *(She plays.)* Now the second one. *(She plays.)* Good, now play the first one and hold the keys down and count eins, zwei, drei, vier. *(She plays.)*

Good now play the second one and hold eins, zwei, drei, vier. *(She plays.)* Good. Now together we can play. Play the first one and hold it while I play. *(SUSCH plays chord while BLATZ plays the first bar of arpeggios.)* Now play the second one. *(SUSCH plays second chord while BLATZ plays the arpeggios.)* Good. Now let's play it through two times.

SUSCH: Better than 'Chopsticks' this is.

> *Together they play through the first two bars twice.*

BLATZ: Good now you can learn this chord. *(BLATZ plays the first chord from the third bar.)*

> *Cow moos.*

SUSCH: Ach, I must yet milk the cows.

> *SUSCH slips out of BLATZ's arm and rises from the bench.*

Teen, what do you still here?

TEEN: *(Rising.)* Such music…how can a person yet go?

> *Cow moos.*

SUSCH: I must go to that cow music.

> *SUSCH grabs milking pails and exits.*

> *BLATZ plays bars from his new sonata, softly. TEEN looks out the window, then pulling herself together, strides over to the piano.*

TEEN: Mensch, what do you in this house with another man's wife?

BLATZ: Klavier spielen! Have not you ears?

TEEN: Knows Obrum how you sit with your arm around his Susch?

BLATZ: Der Kehler has me brought here to learn Susch to play Klavier.

TEEN: And a Klavier teacher must live in the same house with his pupil? Is that how it is in Russia?

BLATZ: Der Beethoven lived often with his pupils in the same house.

TEEN: Even when the pupil was another man's wife?

BLATZ: A composer serves the patron by learning his family to play—daughter, son, wife.

TEEN: Nah yoh, then for sure you could easy learn a patron's friend to play.

> *TEEN sits on the piano bench and snuggles up to him. BLATZ inches away.*

BLATZ: What mean you?

TEEN: Here, now put your arm around and show where the fingers must go.

BLATZ: Aber nein, I cannot.

TEEN: What is loose? I am a woman. I have fingers.

> *TEEN plays a few notes of 'Chopsticks'.*

BLATZ: Nein, nein, die Kunst is not Kinderspiel.

TEEN: Aber spiel with another man's wife yes? Is Kunst?

BLATZ: You have not understanding. A composer seeks revelation.

TEEN: If such a grossartig composer you are, how come it is that you live like a wood tick off the goodness of these people in this poor house?

BLATZ: Fräulein, der Obrum has asked me in. His bidding I do.

TEEN: And you think not if his bidding is right or wrong?

             BLATZ plays the noisy opening bars from 'Moonlight Sonata' third movement, then stops and rises.

BLATZ: Now yet you are casting stones? You yourself are not without sin.

TEEN: What mean you?

BLATZ: You are midwife, not?

TEEN: Yes.

BLATZ: A midwife who helps her friend to meet a man who has suffered terrible mumps.

TEEN: What has that to do with you sleeping under this roof?

BLATZ: Feel you not what this woman wants? And Obrum too?

TEEN: Ach you Mensch, and what want you?

             SUSCH enters. TEEN retreats to the kitchen as SUSCH sets down pails beside the separator.

SUSCH: Still here you are, Teen? The sun is going under.

             BLATZ sits at piano, stares at the sheet music, then very quietly plays from his new sonata.

             SUSCH straightens up and stretches, displaying a small bulge in her belly. TEEN notices, visibly tries to control her alarm.

TEEN: *(Softly.)* You look like you are bettering yourself.

SUSCH: What mean you?

TEEN: Susch, I am your friend. You can tell me.

SUSCH: What?

TEEN: Is Obrum happy?

SUSCH: Obrum is…working away.

TEEN: Oh yes, that is so.

SUSCH: Stay for supper.

TEEN: It's too late now. I must go.

> *TEEN exits.*

> *SUSCH caresses her belly.*

SUSCH: *(Whisper.)* She knows it now, and she would not stay for supper. *(She twitches.)* Ach, but I feel a kick. *(SUSCH smiles, pats her belly, and moves in time to Blatz's playing from his new sonata.)* Will Obrum too see it when for Sunday he comes home?

> *BLATZ stops playing, turns to gaze at SUSCH, begins to rise. SUSCH returns his gaze for a moment, then as if startled, she picks up milk pail and pours milk into the separator reservoir, and begins turning the crank. BLATZ nods his head in time to the cranking and plays again.*

Scene 3

> *Summer. Washline.*

> *SUSCH is obviously pregnant, clothespin apron resting on her protruding belly. TEEN is helping her hang clothes. TEEN's midwife bag on the ground.*

TEEN: True or not the village tongues have something to flap about. You can't hide here and wish just that it will go away.

SUSCH: Why would I want my child to go away? Believe you those lies too?

TEEN: No, I don't…Susch, you must make Blatz go away, you must make things right with Obrum.

SUSCH: What isn't right with me and Obrum? My man works hard so he can build me a new house...what?

TEEN: Just believe me this.

SUSCH: But where can he go?

TEEN: Away! He is not your child! *(Pause.)* Just make Blatz go away.

> *SUSCH sets down the basket and cradles her belly. During the following speech SUSCH is speaking to TEEN but in her emotional turmoil she is unaware that she is making a confession. TEEN reacts physically to SUSCH's words, but cannot speak.*

SUSCH: Yes, it maybe would be better if Blatz went away... poof like a dandelion gone to seed. But so simple it never is...with people... But what's loose with that Obrum? Must I draw for him a picture? On Sundays I think he will say something or ask at least and he just tells about building elevators and now an annex yet or he sleeps in the shade. Maybe when the baby cries already he will see it then. *(Pause.)* Ach Mensch what...what will be if...what if...this baby...who will it look like? If it likens Obrum everything is covered over, not? Covered over with fresh white snow. But if it likens Blatz... holem de gruel...what will Obrum say? What will he do? How will I look him in the eye with that?

> *Faint sound of Model T.*

Obrum comes home. Oh Mensch, to look into his face—no I will febeizel my brain. I am not ready.

> *SUSCH rushes off.*

TEEN: Holem de gruel, my Susch, what can be done? *(She looks around.)* I'll chase him away myself.

> *TEEN storms into the house.*

Blatz, you weasel—

She realizes BLATZ in not there. Sound of someone approaching; TEEN hides behind piano.

OBRUM enters and sets two grocery bags on the table. He pulls a banana out of a bag, peels it partway, bites off the tip and chews as he looks around.

OBRUM: Nah yoh, Suschkje, where hide you that little belly? You say me nothing but I have eyes to see.

OBRUM glances toward Beethoven's piano room.

It's not like we needed him in the end…

He drops the banana peel into the slop pail and enters BLATZ's piano room. TEEN steps from behind the piano.

Teen, what—?

TEEN: Obrum, listen…

OBRUM: What Teen?

TEEN: Obrum, that stormy night…

OBRUM: Yes, you slept with Susch in our bed.

TEEN: Yes, the second time I came, yes…

OBRUM: What mean you, the second time?

TEEN: I came first to bring Susch the dress and…

OBRUM: And what?

TEEN: The house was dark.

OBRUM: But where…in the storm?

TEEN: I know not…I saw no lantern light in the barn, but…

OBRUM: But what?

TEEN: I think I heard...a cry, maybe...

OBRUM: Went you not into the house?

TEEN: Nah well, with all your mumps talk maybe I would be in the way.

OBRUM: But Teen, when I came home after the storm Susch was so dringent lostijch the frost on the windows melted.

TEEN: A woman can have dringent wanting.

OBRUM: And then so soon her belly ached in the morning.

TEEN: Susch said you that?

OBRUM: A husband needs not to be said everything.

TEEN: All is well then...here away from the village.

OBRUM: Well sure...

TEEN: But still your wife you leave here alone with Blatz.

OBRUM: I give a suffering friend a home. *(Pause.)* Und die Musik...such a Mensch we need. To be his patron... it is a small thing. *(Pause.)* He teaches Susch piano.

TEEN: And learns she to play?

OBRUM: What?

TEEN: Matters it not that the village tongues have something to flap about?

OBRUM: Village tongues flap and the rooster crows on the manure pile.

TEEN: So you have what you wanted.

OBRUM: Nah...*(TEEN and OBRUM stare into each other's eyes. OBRUM is without a comeback.)*

TEEN: So send Blatz away. It's not like you needed him in the end. *(TEEN looks around.)* Ach hiet, I must yet to Buhrs. It is Elsie's time.

    TEEN exits.

OBRUM: How can I ask Susch such a thing? Knew I then my meaning? Know I it now? Must I know it? Susch will have a child. We will have a child. Argued Joseph with Mary? Gott im Himmel, is not the child his gift? Aber…

    OBRUM sits at the piano and plays a few notes of 'Chopsticks', then gazes straight ahead, lost in thought.

Scene 4

    Prairie field.

    BLATZ and SUSCH enter from opposite sides.

SUSCH: You? Can't a woman walk alone?

BLATZ: But Sonya.

SUSCH: Enough with that Sonya already!

BLATZ: Uh, Susch, hear once you this, the sounds—

SUSCH: Just noise.

BLATZ: Hear this steppe, this prairie.

SUSCH: Just plaguing noise!

BLATZ: Hear the wind in this grass, the meadowlark.

SUSCH: I believe you nothing.

BLATZ: Just before I spied you walking like a vision from Heaven I saw a small snake.

SUSCH: Snake? Maybe yet an apple too?

BLATZ: The snake made a sound so soft…like a violin played without the bow altogether touching the strings. And I saw a nest on the ground.

SUSCH: Snakes' nest?

BLATZ: No, birds' eggs warming in the sun. Almost I could hear birds singing already in the shell.

SUSCH: What do you with me?

BLATZ: Liebe Sonya, ich muss, I must.

SUSCH: Obrum will see us. Go away!

BLATZ: We can go where the grass is higher…behind the pepper bushes.

SUSCH: What will you with me? Obrum will come.

BLATZ: I feel new music, I feel a new movement for the sonata…come.

SUSCH: Let me go, let go my hand. Go away!

BLATZ: Your hand is music too. Soft music with a rushing of blood. Sonya, Susch, Liebchen you are my muse, not?

SUSCH: What mean you, muse?

BLATZ: Ah Susch, you are the summer prairie all moving, alive, how you say, throbbing.

SUSCH: No, I cannot, not again, I will have a child, I cannot again. Obrum.

BLATZ: Hear once you this, die Harmonie, like angel choir, ja, a symphony…who would think to hear orchestra here on this empty land. Liebchen, I cannot stop. Unheard melody is not sweeter, no… melody I hear…oh he who has ears to hear let him hear!

SUSCH: Blatz no. It is not right, I cannot again. Never again. Even if maybe...I would want...another...no I cannot!

BLATZ: I cannot stop. I must, it must not be lost. *(Releases SUSCH.)* Let me rest on this stone. My pencil, my journal, the notes must be set down. Ich muss schreiben!

SUSCH: Aber what? Now want you to write? And I am just your empty page that you spritz full with ink?

BLATZ: *(Like a mourning dove.)* La, ti, so, so, so.

> *BLATZ furiously writes down the notes he is hearing in his head.*

SUSCH: *(Aside.)* Poof! My brain flies apart like dandelion seeds...always he leaves me with wanting... wanting with him to go to that place where he hears the music.

> *SUSCH gapes at BLATZ in awe, then pulls the picture from her apron. She stares at it for a second.*

You Mensch you, you think such a gift you are, you...you hear once you this...you must leave me so the snow can cover it over.

> *SUSCH rips the picture in half. BLATZ doesn't notice. Shocked, SUSCH shoves the pieces back into her pocket and turns away.*

Sonya I will not be! Aber if Obrum...if Blatz...alone I would be. *(SUSCH caresses her belly in response to a kick.)* Ach, no! He must go!

> *SUSCH exits.*

> *BLATZ writes a few more notes, then jumps up holding his notebook high.*

BLATZ: A man must reach higher than what he can grasp. *(Pause.)* What...what said that woman? A child she said? And she said, "Even if I would want another?" What? A muse that has desire also! Will such a woman send me away? I must write, I must write.

BLATZ writes as he pirouettes.

TEEN enters.

TEEN: Oh, but not a Gypsy yet dancing in the pepper bushes.

BLATZ: Ah, Frau...Fräulein Schellenberg, I saw you not coming.

TEEN: Have you no shame?

BLATZ: Shame?

TEEN: See you not the mischief that you do?

BLATZ: What mean you mischief?

TEEN: Susch...she is...she will have—

BLATZ: Ah, die Susch, die Kunst, die Musik. Ich muss schreiben.

BLATZ pirouettes and writes in his notebook.

TEEN: You must go. These are people...Menschen.

BLATZ: Nah ja, Menschen they are. Not kangaroos. No not kangaroos.

TEEN: Du domma Spucht! Feel you nothing?

BLATZ: Diese Menschen...they receive what they are wanting!

TEEN: And you care not what sorrow will come if you stay here?

BLATZ: Sorrow will come only from your flapping tongue. The music is more worthy than gossip.

BLATZ exits.

TEEN: Am I yet wrong? See I only through my own wanting? But my wanting cannot be...no...not in this world. *(She pauses, smiles.)* Yet how my wanting swells when my dringent Susch grasps what she must have. Susch and her happiness is all. For that Blatz must go!

TEEN exits.

Scene 5

Kitchen and piano room. OBRUM playing 'Chopsticks' softly.

OBRUM: If it happened, would not she bear false witness about herself? *(Pause.)* And if it didn't happen... want I such questions to ask? Wouldn't it be handy if this Russian was just gone home to Russia. But so simple it isn't. A man's head is not stone between the ears. A man's head is thinking, wanting, and seeing what could be. A woman's head too. *(He pauses, smiles.)* Susch's happiness is all. Must the Devil's questions kill her joy?

SUSCH enters, worked up, stops when she sees the grocery bag on the table. She peeks inside, then pulls out a banana, peels it halfway and bites off the tip and rummages in the bag with her free hand as she chews. She pulls out a licorice strap. OBRUM's playing rises in tempo and volume.

SUSCH: Obrum, you shuzzel!

SUSCH stomps into the piano room brandishing the banana and the licorice strap.

All the time such plaguing noise! Send that Blatz away before he turns yet a stick into a snake

OBRUM: Susch, your face is red. Have you a fever?

SUSCH: No, keep your hands at home.

OBRUM: Two weeks I haven't seen you, now you are sick. Want you to lie down?

SUSCH: Leave me alone. No.

> *SUSCH slaps OBRUM with the licorice strap.*

OBRUM: Ow…I brought you that thing to eat.

SUSCH: Just send that Blatz away.

OBRUM: Well sure, I'll send Blatz away. But first let me feel you around with my arms. I get so lonesome in Gretna.

> *SUSCH slaps OBRUM again with the licorice strap.*

SUSCH: No, let me go! I am not a cat for men to stroke!

OBRUM: But Susch, you always liked this, not?

SUSCH: Shuft, let me go—no don't touch me there. The baby.

OBRUM: What?

SUSCH: Even a blind man would see that I will have a baby.

OBRUM: Well, sure, I see that.

SUSCH: You know?

OBRUM: Yeah sure, but is something loose with the baby?

SUSCH: What could be loose with the baby?

OBRUM: You never said nothing to me.

SUSCH: Nah well…you said me that I would have a baby…I mean…you always know everything best and you brought me a…

OBRUM: The rocking chair you mean?

SUSCH: Uh yoh, and besides you are always away.

OBRUM: *(Embracing her.)* I am home now.

SUSCH: No don't.

OBRUM: Can't a father feel it too?

SUSCH: What?

OBRUM: A father wants to feel his baby too.

SUSCH: I-I never thought.

OBRUM: If I hold here will he kick my hand?

SUSCH: He kicks not always the same place. He waits till I am busy and then, shtooks. I never know where it will come.

OBRUM: I sure would like to feel it.

SUSCH: It would be so good if you would stay home.

OBRUM: Yes, I almost have enough to build the house.

SUSCH: And you will send Blatz away? And the piano too?

OBRUM: Yeah sure, and then it will be just us and the baby. Was that a kick there by my hand?

SUSCH: Yes, almost like little toes stroking wet grass. Sometimes when Blatz plays piano real quiet I feel the baby's toes stroking like that, or maybe little fingers, what you think? Can a baby in the belly hear piano playing?

OBRUM: Could be, maybe. Anyways Blatz will be gone. I will tell him to go.

SUSCH: Where can such a man go?

OBRUM: We do not have to keep him. The child—

SUSCH: Maybe music is good for a baby.

OBRUM: Blatz is not our child...Susch, yes, I must tell him to go, he belongs not here with us...we have our own family to make...and I will build you a warm house.

SUSCH: Will it hold out the windy tongues flapping themselves tired over what kind of nest we have here away from the village? *(Pause.)* What kind of nest have we anyways?

OBRUM: Nest? We have you and me on our own land, and there will be a baby.

SUSCH: And we have a Blatz too in this grain shed house. Why leave you me alone with that Blatz anyways?

OBRUM: He suffers still. His piano playing is the only repair for his wounded heart.

SUSCH: He plays not now! He mumbles over the field, 'Hear once you this, hear once you this.'

            OBRUM tries to embrace her.

OBRUM: Blatz hears music in this place.

            SUSCH slaps OBRUM's cheek with the licorice strap.

            BLATZ enters in a composition trance, oblivious to SUSCH and OBRUM as he sits down at the piano and begins to try out fragments from his notebook on the piano. SUSCH and OBRUM watch in awe.

            BLATZ plays a bar.

BLATZ: Bitte, hear once you this. *(Plays it again.)*

SUSCH: No

                    SUSCH stomps out.

BLATZ: Hear once you this. *(Plays again.)* Ach, mein dummer Herr. Unheard melodies are sweeter. Why I cannot do it right? I must, oh let me try this. *(Plays.)* Better, little bit, ja? *(Plays.)*

OBRUM: Blatz, you must tell me this already.

BLATZ: *(Plays.)* Hear once you this.

OBRUM: Blatz, you can see I think, that Susch is—

BLATZ: Hear once you this. *(Plays.)* This arpeggio here, is it too much Beethoven? *(Plays it again.)*

OBRUM: You are Beethoven Blatz, not? And you must tell it to me already, did you...Susch, see, she will soon...I must know this thing.

BLATZ: Hear once you this. *(Plays mourning dove trill.)* Mourning dove not? On a violin it would be better...music must have hammering and stroking to be full, stroking and hammering, blowing too sometimes...ach what kind of God made us so we would make instruments?

OBRUM: What has it to do with God? Mensch, say it already what you have done with my Susch. I must know if you achieved the harmonie with Susch. Stroking, hammering, blowing, I must know this.

BLATZ: Ach, a Mensch is never satisfied with what he can grasp and so he picks up a stick. That is what makes us gods too, not?

OBRUM: Blatz, I must know this.

BLATZ: Obrum Kehler, mein dummer Herr. You picked up

	a stick to reach where you could not grasp. Did not you get what you wanted?
OBRUM:	Well sure, maybe…but…
BLATZ:	Bitte, hear once you this. *(Plays.)*
OBRUM:	Blatz, what is yet to come, how will I…how will you live?
BLATZ:	Listen. *(Plays.)* Hear the prairie?
OBRUM:	Blatz, I hear it said that in Gnadenthal village…a teacher they are looking for. And in Gnadenthal those people sing and play instruments there.
BLATZ:	This Klavier I must have.
OBRUM:	But Blatz, what want you here with this broken piano that even God himself can't keep in tune? Why want you to stay here in this grain shed? Could not a musician find opportunity in Winkler or Winnipeg even?
BLATZ:	Obrum, this wounded instrument is my stick. Without it I have no reach.
OBRUM:	Then accept this piano as my gift and go.
BLATZ:	My patron, you understand not the muse. I must have this virgin steppe, this humble house, and *(Whispers.)* for my gift to you, my patron, I shall have payment.
OBRUM:	Payment?
BLATZ:	Requested you not a tuned instrument?
OBRUM:	The piano.
BLATZ:	Say you now that I did not grasp your meaning?
OBRUM:	Grasp my meaning now! In two weeks I return to build the new house. This grain shed can be for

burning. *(OBRUM smashes his fist on the keys.)* And this Klavier also!

OBRUM exits.

BLATZ: Sturm und Drang, Sturm und Drang. Aber with fire to play…nein, in two weeks my sonata notes must be fixed. *(Plays.)* Aber if I should hear stirring another sonata…*(Plays.)* Winkler? Winnipeg? More frightful schools.

Scene 6

Two weeks later. Yard. Kitchen. Piano room.

SUSCH, big as a house pregnant, waddles toward the house carrying two pails of milk. BLATZ plays his Susch sonata, stumbling less frequently than he has before. SUSCH sets down her pails to rest.

SUSCH: *(Sighs.)* Just maybe once those long fingers could milk the cows?

BLATZ stops and replays a few bars that involve the off-key keys. He changes the fingering so as to avoid the off keys without marring the flow of the music. SUSCH plays an imaginary piano.

BLATZ: Ach ja, Sonya, it goes yet, yes, it goes yet when a man changes his thrust, changes the slant yes, the tilt, the aim, it can be done Sonya, it can be done, a man can reach even with a broken stick, ja Sonya, almost your bow I can feel on the strings, almost your bow I can hear—such legatissimo, such arpeggios, such stroking between the hammering of the keys, ach Herr Ludwig must this way have felt when he played the Kreutzer. Who played violin for him? Had he a Sonya too?

BLATZ plays on, losing himself in a reverie of lost steppes. SUSCH catches herself in mid-movement, laughs, picks up the pails and carries them into the house.

She pours one pail into the reservoir, sets the empty pail down, but instead of turning the crank she begins nodding her head in time to BLATZ's music. BLATZ is in fine form, playing without stumbling. SUSCH swaying in time to the music makes her way to the Brummtopp and in her reverie runs her fingers through the horsehair.

SUSCH: *(Sighing.)* Yes...yes...yes, my child. *(Aside.)* Your music flies, but you stay in this poor nest. Will not the air hold up your wings?

BLATZ stumbles on a few notes.

BLATZ: A violin I need. *(Backtracks, stumbles again.)* Or a cello, something low.

He begins pounding the keys in one of his characteristic rages. SUSCH is startled out of her reverie.

SUSCH: No wait! Listen you Mensch!

SUSCH dips her hands in water, pulls the horsehair swatch taut and rubs the hair between her fingers and gets a rhythmic rumbling sound going, a jerking, nudging rhythm, like a bird pushing a fledgling from a nest.

BLATZ stops pounding the keys, cocks his ear, plays a chord that resonates with the Brummtopp. SUSCH lets rip a few more "snorts", then drops the horsehair and slips onto the bench beside BLATZ. She reaches across his lap and plays the opening chord from 'Moonlight Sonata' he taught her earlier. Without thinking BLATZ plays the arpeggio.

Now fix your song.

BLATZ: What mean...ah ja...*(He plays the troublesome phrase, revising as he goes.)* ah Sonya, so simple this woman isn't—

SUSCH: Susch, mein kleiner Beethoven, ich bin Susch.

BLATZ: Na ja Liebchen, ich weiss, aber…what? Beethoven she calls me.

BLATZ embraces SUSCH.

SUSCH: Tell me Beethoven where you go.

BLATZ: Go? I go no place, I stay here. Always. I have no auto, I have no horse.

SUSCH: Nein, nein! Where go you when…when you hear once you this with that music?

BLATZ: What mean you, where go I? *(Aside.)* Sonya, how can I say it to this woman?

SUSCH wrenches out of the embrace and rises.

SUSCH: Dummkopp, say it me already, where go you when you hear the music?

BLATZ: Ach Son…Susch, how to say it, the place I go is a…I have not words…sackcloth and ashes…gnashing of teeth…yet also mourning dove, meadowlark, sparrow…a hellish heaven it is, Sonya…Susch.

SUSCH: Beethoven, is there truth in such a place?

BLATZ: Truth?

SUSCH: Wahrheit. No lies. Your music, it is true?

BLATZ: Ich weiss nicht. Es ist compliziert.

SUSCH: For sure, complicated it is.

BLATZ: *(Rising from bench.)* Sonya, Susch, die Musik, not such a simplistic thing, und ich…der Kehler…aber such beauty drives the music…a composer needs Eros…

SUSCH: What means that?

BLATZ: Straumheit, Lust, ah, Aphrodite, Venus.

SUSCH: Wonder you not who this baby will liken?

BLATZ: Oh...that...matters such a thing?

SUSCH: (*In a hoarse, desperate whisper.*) Blatz, Beethoven Blatz, how can you...how can you yet hear such music...in the birds, in the grass, even yet in a snake...and then yet ask "matters such a thing"?

BLATZ: Was meinst du?

SUSCH: Haben sie kein Herz? How can you yet make music that confuses my heart, clappers my bones, and yes, mein dummer Herr, tickles me like maybe a snake in the grass and lifts me from bread dough in the pan up to white clouds in the sky, and you wonder not who this baby will liken?

BLATZ: Son...Susch, ich...I know not what.

SUSCH: Tell me once this, why played you with my weakness?

BLATZ: Der Kehler...he mumbled about mumps...and your wanting...he gave me to understand.

        SUSCH grabs BLATZ by the shoulders.

SUSCH: Der Kehler gave you to understand?

BLATZ: Die Muzik...das Klavier...die—

SUSCH: And I mean nothing?

BLATZ: You reached. (*Pause.*) Liebe Susch, du bist die Muzik.

        SUSCH collapses against BLATZ, who holds her awkwardly.

SUSCH: I think I will febeizel my brain.

OBRUM enters.

OBRUM: Huy yuy yuy, what gives with this? Was such my meaning?

SUSCH: *(In a daze.)* Du bist die Musik? Der Kehler gave him to understand? *(Sees OBRUM.)* Obrum, what have—

TEEN stomps in, axe in hand, heading straight for the piano.

OBRUM: Teen!

BLATZ shields SUSCH.

TEEN: Blatz, you will go! Susch cannot have such a shadow on her child!

TEEN raises the axe. OBRUM grabs the axe from behind. TEEN and OBRUM struggle.

SUSCH: *(Oblivious.)* You gave him to understand?

TEEN: Obrum, let me go

OBRUM: No Teen!

TEEN: I must destroy this thing so the child can live! Such shame Susch has not earned.

OBRUM: No! Blatz help!

BLATZ grabs TEEN and holds her so OBRUM can wrench the axe from her grip.

TEEN: Let me go, you high-nosed Russian!

SUSCH: I reached—ow, ow, OW!

SUSCH doubles over clutching her belly.

OBRUM: Susch, what's loose?

SUSCH: I reached...Ow!

SUSCH sinks to the floor.

OBRUM: Blatz, help!

OBRUM rushes to help SUSCH, but is uncertain what to do. BLATZ, releases TEEN, but fears to take action. TEEN stares blankly.

SUSCH: To the bed, help me already to the bed!

OBRUM: For sure, the bed. Blatz help.

BLATZ: The feet or the head?

OBRUM: What mean you?

SUSCH: Help me just to stand and I will walk to the bed!

OBRUM and BLATZ collide as they grab for SUSCH's shoulders.

Don't step on me yet!

BLATZ: Water! On the floor

SUSCH: My water has broken!

OBRUM: Broken water?

SUSCH: To the bed, hurry.

OBRUM and BLATZ lift SUSCH to her feet and help her stumble to the bedroom where they help her settle in the bed.

TEEN returns to reality and hurries over to the bed.

TEEN: Blatz, Obrum, heraus! Boil water!

BLATZ and OBRUM rush to kitchen, collide trying to get the kettle onto the stove. OBRUM braces himself on the stove.

OBRUM: Cold. Blatz make fire.

BLATZ: I will.

> *BLATZ slips away and sits at the piano.*

OBRUM: Make fire, I said.

BLATZ: Hear once you this! It burns, not?

> *BLATZ plays opening chords of SUSCH sonata. Stops.*

OBRUM: Blatz, what you do?

SUSCH: *(From bedroom.)* Obrum come!

> *OBRUM enters the bedroom. SUSCH arches her back with the pain of a contraction.*

Your spoon too this borscht has stirred.

OBRUM: What mean you?

SUSCH: Ow...ow...he wants not out in the world.

> *SUSCH reaches out to OBRUM. OBRUM clumsily takes her hand and stands there completely confused. SUSCH grips his hand and yanks him toward her so that he almost tumbles onto the bed, but he manages to brace himself against the head railing so he is hovering over SUSCH in an awkward stance.*

TEEN: Susch, you are having a baby!

SUSCH: It feels good to keep him.

OBRUM: Gott im Himmel, what mean you?

SUSCH: Ow...ow...push him I must, but if he cannot, will not fly—ow, ow—

TEEN: Obrum out! This is women's business.

SUSCH: Oh Obrum, wondered you not?

OBRUM: Wondered what?

SUSCH: Likening.

OBRUM: Likening what?

SUSCH: Ach Obrum, you…ow…ow.

TEEN: Out now! Susch has work to do! Out! *(Aside to OBRUM.)* Make Blatz go!

SUSCH: Ow!

> *OBRUM leaves and approaches BLATZ at the piano.*

(Calling.) Play me that sonata!

BLATZ: *(Plays a few bars.)* The sonata, it stumbles not so much now, yes. *(Plays on.)* Can you hear it?

OBRUM: Mensch, take up your broken piano and walk!

BLATZ: Care you not where I go? *(Repeats a bar and plays on.)*

OBRUM: Go to Gretna, go to Russia, just go!

> *BLATZ repeats a bar adding a new trill then stops abruptly and grabs for his manuscript.*

BLATZ: Schnell, I must write this now!

OBRUM: Blatz you must go!

BLATZ: Mein dummer Kehler, know you not that the music nears completion?

OBRUM: Your piano is just a plaguing noise.

BLATZ: Wonder you not whom this baby will liken? Wondered you not about that when you threw the cabbage into the pot?

OBRUM: You think you are such a gift from God himself, you plaguing noise. For sure this baby will liken me.

BLATZ:	And if it likens the true father?
OBRUM:	I am the true father.
BLATZ:	Ach ja, mein dummer Herr. *(BLATZ plays a thundering bar.)* Such is the harmony.
SUSCH:	Gott im Himmel! Obrum come!

OBRUM rushes to her side.

TEEN:	Sh...sh...it will pass.
SUSCH:	We have something done.
OBRUM:	We?
SUSCH:	I and you. We two.
OBRUM:	What?
SUSCH:	Ow! Why is it such hellish hurting?
TEEN:	Susch, it will pass.
SUSCH:	Such hellish wanting a woman should not have.
TEEN:	God's nature it is, they say, aber...
SUSCH:	If God's nature it is, then—ow, ow!
TEEN:	Sh...sh...you are not alone in your wanting.
SUSCH:	Obrum, why brought you that piano and that Blatz?
OBRUM:	Die Musik.
SUSCH:	Why did you?
OBRUM:	So you can learn.
SUSCH:	Me? Me who cannot coo even back to a mourning dove?
TEEN:	Keep still, wait for the next pain.

SUSCH: Why did you leave me alone with Blatz?

OBRUM: Blatz said me that learning is better when no other ears hear fingers stumble.

SUSCH: Knew you not my wanting when you brought me Blatz?

OBRUM: Nah, well, I thought so the piano…

SUSCH: Obrum lie not now! Gave you Blatz to understand?

OBRUM: Understand?

SUSCH: You saw a rainbow in a snowstorm.

OBRUM: Rainbow?

SUSCH: *(Laughs.)* Oh but yes, when people get hartsoft dringent for something—

OBRUM: But no!

SUSCH: *(Laughing.)* Obrum you always know everything best. Ow, ow. Why did you Teen?

TEEN: Sh…

SUSCH: Why played you with my wanting?

TEEN: What mean you?

SUSCH: Why did you say me things about Obrum's mumps?

TEEN: I saw your wanting…I saw Obrum's wanting… aber Susch, believe me this, I was covering over only my own hellish wanting when I joked about a Gypsy in the hayloft after Obrum said to me how he feared the mumps had—

SUSCH: Ow…ow…

TEEN: Soon…soon…soon.

OBRUM:	Susch, Susch, Blatz will go and we will have what we want.

OBRUM rushes over to BLATZ at the piano.

SUSCH:	*(Moans.)*
OBRUM:	Blatz go, you must.
BLATZ:	No, I cannot.
OBRUM:	I am Susch's husband.
BLATZ:	Ja, a husband who hires a man to learn his wife to play.
OBRUM:	Surely such you would not say.
BLATZ:	Die Musik kommt dan auch vom Leben.
OBRUM:	You have music made from…?
BLATZ:	Hear once you this, the sonata it has Resonanz, not. *(Plays.)* Wanting and reaching. A stick, ja. *(Plays.)* Aber yet little bit thin.
OBRUM:	You phony Beethoven. You Katzenjammer camel nose.
SUSCH:	*(Cries out.)*
TEEN:	Push!

TEEN holds up the baby.

A son you have.

SUSCH:	Good, but does he have a mother? I feel all hollowed out.
TEEN:	You are still all here. Nothing is lost.
SUSCH:	Likens he…?
TEEN:	Here look.

SUSCH: I'm frightened to look, is he…?

TEEN: Here.

SUSCH: Oh. *(Pause.)* But yes, it is best this way.

TEEN: Time to call in your man.

SUSCH: Obrum, yes.

TEEN: *(Calling.)* Obrum.

            OBRUM comes over.

            You have a son.

            SUSCH hands the baby to OBRUM. The baby gurgles.

OBRUM: He looks…

TEEN: He looks like his mother the way God wants it.

            BLATZ begins to play the Susch sonata. The baby gurgles and falls asleep. OBRUM returns the baby, sits on the edge of the bed, takes SUSCH's hand and gazes at the sleeping baby cradled in her arms.

OBRUM: What will we do?

SUSCH: Just keep the top full and the bottom clean.

OBRUM: *(Whispers.)* No, I mean what will we with Beethoven Blatz?

SUSCH: Hear you that music?

OBRUM: Yoh, sure.

SUSCH: *(Talking to herself.)* He needs not much.

OBRUM: What mean you?

SUSCH: *(Still talking to herself.)*…what music could be if we send him…

OBRUM: Yes, send him—

SUSCH: (*Still talking to herself.*) …but in this grain shed house…the music would be like a belly full with growing…and now and then a shtooks—

TEEN: But no, your son!

OBRUM: You cannot want this.

SUSCH: (*Still talking to herself.*) He is not my child. Must I make him fly?

OBRUM: What?

SUSCH: Blatz come!

TEEN: No!

> *BLATZ slinks in. SUSCH holds up the baby.*

SUSCH: The child is born. Here, hold him.

> *Gingerly BLATZ reaches for the baby and holds it close to his face. The baby screams blue murder. BLATZ hastily returns the baby to SUSCH's arms.*

Beethoven Blatz, bring your sonatas into the world. Go…where you must…go…where you hear the music. (*Pause.*) Aber bitte spiel wieder Klavier.

> *Relieved BLATZ returns to the piano and begins to play the Susch sonata. The baby calms.*

Obrum, the new house you can finish before winter?

OBRUM: (*Caresses her cheek.*) For sure, and I brought a washing machine with this load.

SUSCH: Thank you, Obrum. The piano can stay in this grain shed house…ready. (*To TEEN.*) I feel your wanting, my dear dear friend. (*SUSCH reaches for*

TEEN's hand. TEEN sits on bed.) Thank you Teen for bringing me Obrum…Obrum who brings me things.

> *TEEN kisses SUSCH's hand. For a moment all three listen to BLATZ's playing.*

TEEN: All can be well then, here away from the village.

> *TEEN rises from the bed and moves to the Brummtopp beside the piano. She wets her hands and picks up the horsehair, listens to BLATZ's playing, then begins to rub the hair until she achieves a rhythmic thrum. BLATZ stops playing, hands suspended as he listens for the resonance. TEEN alters the tone. BLATZ drops his hands to the keys and begins to play in harmony with TEEN. TEEN catches on and the two continue to play, each in turn, leading and following the other.*

OBRUM: A nest, my Susch, full with love and music.

> *BLATZ's piano playing fades out. TEEN alters the rhythm of the Brummtopp. BLATZ rises from the piano and takes a few steps toward the door, pauses, gazes at OBRUM, SUSCH, and the BABY on the bed, then slinks back to the piano.*

BLATZ: *(Sings to tune of 'Ode to Joy'.)*
                Sonatas too are born from living
                Passions burning still by half

SUSCH: *(Joins in.)*
                Earth cherries from husks are giving

OBRUM: *(Joins in.)*
                Coo to the mourning dove and laugh.

TEEN: *(Joins in.)*
                Wanting, reaching, hearts confusing
                Flapping tongues will fan the chaff

Shadows loom dark o'er our choosing
Coo to the mourning dove and laugh.

BLATZ plays a chord. The baby screams in a rage.

The End.